The contents of this book, while based on fact, are written from my own recollections of events that took place on the 15th April 2000 and the subsequent years.

It is our story. However, our story is not unique as thousands of people, black and white were persecuted during the volatile land invasions.

We were part of a courageous community that stood in solidarity and defiance against the violence associated to the ever present winds of change that swept through the farming world.

While there are many incidences that took place during these turbulent years not mentioned, they are not forgotten.

1

Copyright © Jenny Luke 2018

ISBN: 9781723960888
Imprint: Independently published

Dancing In The Storm

With the sun slipping quietly behind the hill and the sweet breath of evening closing in, I strain my ears, listening intently, and on a couple of occasions I am convinced I can hear the hoarse cough of the female leopard. From the water way and the garden, the twilight orchestra vibrates gently through the golden dusk; a perfect swansong, before the sun takes its final bow, falling gently below the horizon.

PROLOGUE

A racing event is attracting thousands of people and the road is a bumper to bumper audio fest. A year after abandoning our sun kissed corner of the world, we are still struggling to identify with this new life; its traffic madness and the pandemonium of urban living. I open the window an inch, hoping to allure natures' soothing breeze to caress my cheek, but the air is redolent with fumes. The deep drone of a helicopter pulsates in the air and I crane my neck, keeping an eye on the glinting rotor blades dissecting the shafts of sunlight peeping out from behind a gilt edged cloud. From the air, the traffic must resemble mile after mile of an unprotected metallic backbone of many colours as we inch forward nose to tail. The only fast moving traffic is the large throaty motor bikes that weave in and out, racing the wind, whooshing past like space invaders with dark leathers and full faced helmets. With the honking of horns, angry curses and the radio blasting, I long for the peace and quiet of home with the wide open spaces and wild animals. A pang, painfully sharp, like a fist in the gut has me bent over.

Leaning back against the headrest, I allow my thoughts to meander like a stream and the memories flow into my consciousness, teasing my mind with images of msasa trees, vultures and a female leopard. My other life, or the journey that had got me to this exact point on the road, begins to unfold. My eye's droop heavily and my mind travels back in time to a place that my heart pines for; our farm in the Virginia district, Zimbabwe.

Chapter 1

METHVEN RANCH 1995

Sixteen years after independence and the infamous Mugabe speech, which promised a 'Nation of peace and reconciliation?' we are well ensconced in the Zimbabwean farming world adding to the flowing fields of constant growth. Gary, Mikaela, Ben and I finally have what we consider to be the most beautiful, if not the easiest piece of land to farm in the Virginia district, north east of the capital Harare, Zimbabwe. We have been leasing the farm for the past three years, and now, after negotiations with our landlord, we have signed on the dotted line. We now own five thousand acres of what can be described as two sections, the top being a plateau and on good authority, the highest tobacco farm in the country. On this section of the farm, we are 1600m above sea level. I can reach up and touch the cloud wrapped heaven, while the throb of the sunburnt earth trembles beneath my feet. The sunshine spreads like powdered gold over the grassy fields which roll into untamed bush before dropping a thousand foot into the valley where the morning mist rises with summer laziness, enveloping the homestead, workshop and barns.

I leap out of the car on our return from Harare. Life is perfect. The bronze sun gazes down on us and I raise my arms, allowing the rays to slip gently through my fingers. Bending my knees and stomping on a foot, I clap a hand and raise my foot up to make contact with the palm of the opposite hand. Laughing hysterically, I manage a few more uncoordinated leaps, crooking a finger at Gary, enticing him to join in my childish burst of energy. He grins, shaking his head. However, he is happiness: radiating a warmth and passion, the necessary ingredients to build the cornerstones for our future. Sixteen years of hard work has finally paid off.

'We have done it, Gary. It's ours, it's ours.' I have stopped my dyslexic version of the gumboot dance, instead, leaning over resting my hands on my knees, catching my breath.

'Mad as a March hare, Dad.' Ben's index finger traces imaginary circles near his temple as he flashes a cheeky grin at me.

'Happiness is.' I point towards myself, beaming like an idiot. I am fizzing over with excitement, my heart all a flutter in that magical space of achievement. Sixteen years along this purposeful path on our quest for life, Adam, our gardener has been at our sides, green fingers creating another beautiful haven. He peers around the corner, cupping his hands together and grinning widely as his future is now secure. He will work until his hair turns grey, before taking on lighter duties in the garden.

Maggie, our maid of ten years is crooning to the fish in the fish tank as I enter the kitchen. She taps gently on the glass with her index finger coaxing them to swim towards her; tiny polished jewels glittering in the late afternoon sun. As she becomes aware of my footsteps, she confides to the fish in a whispery tone that we all now have a permanent home. I keep a straight face, while Gary grins, shaking his head. What can I say because I also talk to the dogs, the birds and even the fish; she mirrors me.

'This is home, Jen, and definitely the nut house.' He rolls his eyes towards Maggie before chortling. 'Our lives are perfect. This is the start of our dynasty, Mikaela and Ben.' He is earnest. 'To be passed down for generations to come.' He hugs me tight. Our tune of happiness is accompanied by the soft melodious tinkle from the wind chime outside the kitchen window. The two boxer cross bitches cavort, rumps rolling from side to side, tongues lolling from wide grinning mouths. Maggie smiles, turns away and continues to talk to the fish.

Chapter 2

CONFUSION APRIL 15TH 2000

News Headline: 'WHITE FARMER SHOT DEAD IN ZIMBABWE. FIVE OTHERS ABDUCTED. FARMERS AND THEIR FAMILIES EVACUATE AREA.'

The BBC breaking news bulletin shrieks out from the television glaring at us from the corner in my sister Sue's lounge. The screen offers the only light in the room and the sliver of warmth peeping through from the kitchen casts eerie shadows on the far wall. They appear to gloat as they dance and sway; well in keeping with the day's madness. I slump back into the confines of the thickly padded armchair. Alarm tears and gnaws at my innards like rodents on the prowl. I stare, bleary eyed at the television. The broadcaster's voice penetrates the thick fog in my head, sounding calm and impersonal. A far cry from how I am feeling. The sporadic and intense tightening in my chest is excruciating, like a hand clenching and squeezing my heart; stealing my thoughts and scattering them with careless abandon to the elements.

Mikaela is crouched on the arm of my blue chair. Her toned brown arms are coiled defensively around her jean clad legs; long fingers clenched together, hanging onto hope. Her long blonde hair is scraped away from her face, accentuating her classical cheek bones and large expressive light brown eyes, which are now clouded in darkness. Like me, her smiling mouth and well defined lips dip at the corners, giving her face a sombre look. Her trembling hand creeps

8

into mine and we sit, clammy palms clasped tightly together, unsure of our destiny as we watch the names of the farmers inch their way across the screen.

'Ben. Oh bloody hell, Sue,' I am airborne, reminded once again that I have been unable to make contact with him. 'I need to get hold of our boy. Oh hell, he must not hear the news of his dad like this. Not over the radio or television.' It is 11.00pm and I am shocked that the BBC is broadcasting this story. I have already been informed about the tragedy, but I have been unable to speak to many family members. I feel the blood coursing through my veins and my heart rate charging ahead creating a drum like din in my ears.

The contact number we were given for Ben just rings and rings. I push my limp fringe away from my face in frustration. 'Now Gary's name is on the television and I don't want Ben to hear about his dad in the middle of the night. I can feel my chest heaving in and out. 'Keep your control.' I am muttering under my breath. Panic is my enemy; I fill my lungs, letting the air escape, slowly. Ben is away on a rugby tour with his school. They are playing a variety of different schools down in South Africa. I lean over and turn the side lamp on. The rosy glow does nothing to lift our spirits, but it is better than sitting in the gloom.

I lean back allowing my heavy eye lids to close. What the hell happened today? This morning, life had been normal, or as normal as life for farmers in Zimbabwe could be. Tonight I am listening with my heart in my mouth to the BBC news channel on the television replaying the events that happened in our farming area earlier today. My family's, along with many others' in the farming world is in chaos; manmade chaos. Sue leans over; kissing my forehead gently and I make room for her on the cushion. We both sit quietly and I can feel the steady rhythm of her heart pounding against my shoulder. My mum and dad sit quietly, viewing the scene with distraught expressions marring their normally cheerful faces.

'Mum, what are we going to do?' Mikaela's lips quiver and huge pearl like tears form, glistening as they cascade over her lids.

'We have to sit and wait for news. I am sorry. I don't know what else we can do.' I am out of the chair in an instant and I fold her into my arms. We hug tightly, drawing on each others' energy and warmth. She has been a pillar of strength, taking calls and speaking to friends. I walk with her to the couch and push her gently backwards. Her skin is hot to the touch, but I know that like me she is cold and empty inside. She curls up into a foetal position, clasping her knees tightly, and she sobs with great rasping breaths. Sue sits close to her, stroking the blonde tresses off her face. I lean over and kiss her, trying to erase the aura of trouble that hovers, like a grim halo over her blonde head.

There is a bewilderment pulsing through the air and the atmosphere in the room feels oppressive and wet on my skin. The air clutches me, threatening suffocation and I run outside, gasping and swallowing greedily at the fresh night breeze. I lick my lips, tasting the salt of the evening's tears.

Sue's clock which has stood by our family marking the minutes of our lives, chimes 12 midnight. I stare up at the old intricately laced hands of the clock, watching as they tick slowly, but surely. The minutes go by and there is still no news of Gary and the other men. I think of Ben. I wish he was here with us. I had already decided that it will be best to phone our friends in South Africa at about 5am, and he can speak to Ben's rugby coach before giving him news of his dad. Oh my word, I hope that by morning we will have some news. What are we going to do? My mum and dad have retired with heavy hearts and plodding foot steps to the spare room.

'What started this chain of events this morning, Jen?' Sue steadies my hands with a firm, but kind grip. 'I don't understand how Gary was involved.' Her square jaw line is clenched tightly and her blue grey eyes are intense as she tries to keep me focused.

'Sue, we have been waiting for something to happen for weeks now. The stress of living with these self proclaimed war veterans or war vets squatting on the land has been unbearable. Our nerves are shot. Mugabe has given them carte blanche to invade our land, our lives and the lives of our labour. We all know they need land but my God, not like this. The violence is sickening, and farmers are becoming prisoners on their own farms. The fact that we don't have anybody squatting on Methven Ranch (our farm) does not detract from the tension. We worry about everyone in the district. These land invasions have all been about him garnishing votes.' I wipe a weary hand over my face. My light brown hair hangs limp and lifeless over my forehead. I am locked in the prison of my own fears.

'Jen, I know all that, but what happened this morning?' Sue's voice drags me back from my thoughts.

I stare up at her through blank eyes and still clinging tightly to her hand; she is my raft and if I let go, I feel I might drown in the enormity of the huge political tsunami bearing down on us all. I let my mind wander back in time to the beginning of the year and the events leading up to today's evacuation of the farming district.

Chapter 3

THE NEW MILENNIUM

The glorious orange glow of dawn crests over the fir trees. Golden rays caress the sky, leaves quiver in anticipation of a warm kiss and an explosion of bird calls trill tunefully; embracing the new millennium. The sun chases elongated shadows that look rather like hooded figures, stretching out over the grass; creeping up and through my side window.

'1st January 2000, Gary,' I push my long finger gently into his ribs. 'Happy new year, hon. Can you believe that we are actually waking up in the car on this momentous occasion of the dawning of the new millennium? We are normally the last to leave the party. Do you think that we have finally grown up?' My eyes appear larger as the kohl has smudged slightly, and I open them wide, dripping cool refreshing eye drops in. 'Hide the evidence of some hard partying last night,' I laugh, 'want some?' I offer him the bottle of eye drops.

'No thanks Jen, I'm okay. Well I would say that, we have grown up, just a little bit.' He wipes his eyes and runs a hand through his hair that is as temperamental as an unruly teenager. 'We are waiting for Ben to finish his party, mmm. Should we let him walk? I suppose that would be a bit of lousy stunt to pull after a night long party. No, we will wait and anyway it brings back memories, the two of us in a car!' Gary smiles with a wicked glint in his eye and leaning over, he plants a kiss on my lips, making me chuckle. 'This is going to be our year, Jen. The gods are on our side. I feel it in my bones.' his voice is light and cheery.

'The gods should be on your side after what they threw at you last year.' I take hold of his rough hand, holding it tightly. I frown.

'Hey, are you okay?' He keeps his gaze on me, his dark eyes probing, and I blink at him. His dark brown irises appear to be black, reflecting storm clouds on the horizon.

'I am fine, Gary. We should not tempt fate.' I shiver. 'I just have a few butterflies flapping around in my stomach.' The goose bumps on my arms tingle and I rub them gently. A deep foreboding is so overwhelming, an icy whisper of evil that invokes a strong desire to flee. I glance away, unable to chase away these morbid invaders which are as cold and menacing as crystal lace frost.

January soon passes into February. We are excited and looking forward to the year ahead. Gary's heart attack which happened in June 1999, traumatic and frightening at the time is forgotten news, but not quite so the snapped Achilles heel tendon which befell him in August 1999. One operation and four skin grafts later, his calf looks like a small patchwork cover. It is raw, but much improved. He is incorrigible. I think back to August with a smile. His brown craggy face, mouth turned up in a smile, dark hair peeking out cheekily from his old farm cap and a plaster cast hugging his leg up to the thigh. With a casual wave of the hand he climbs onto his red motor bike.

'Do you want to come with me?' He opens his eyes wide, grinning at me. I refuse. 'I need to go and check on the labour.' He sighs and adjusts his bum, patting the seat behind him.

'Are you stark staring mad, Gary? Ride pillion with you. Look at your leg.' I point at the plaster cast that sticks out at a dreadful angle. 'You look like a good advert for what not to do, when you have a cast up to the hip.'

'Don't be fresh, Jen.'

'Well someone has got to be in one piece around here to drive you to the hospital.' I wave bye. 'If you fall off, just run on home.' I laugh. 1999 had brought nothing but disaster his way. The new millennium is being kind to us and my earlier forebodings have been put on the back burner.

Zimbabwe is once again, gearing up to face another election in June 2000. Robert Mugabe is attempting to change the constitution, and he is calling for a referendum to be held. He is again talking about taking farms without any payment. What is more frightening though is his attempt to hold onto power, and this he will be able to do by changing the constitution. He will give himself absolute power for the remainder of his life.

My mum and dad (who have been resident on the farm for the past couple of years), Gary, Mikaela, Ben and I sit around the dining room table discussing this latest political strategy of Mugabe's. Cleaning my plate and leaning back, I feel replete.

'I think we need to vote in these coming elections.' We all stare at my dad in surprise. As a white community, we have been inclined to leave politics to the African people. 'The time has come now, where we need to make a stand. Mugabe should never have sent the forces to the Congo. God alone knows how much money is wasted there.' Dad thumps the table with his fist. Mugabe had sent 11 000 troops to the Congo in 1998. We don't know too much about it, but feel sure that he must have a finger in the 'blood diamonds', but it is all conjecture. 'I bet it is costing Zimbabwe a fortune funding these troops in the Congo.' My dad has a noisy slurp of his beer, and I laugh at the way he likes to get his pennies worth in. 'I bet he is being paid in blood diamonds too.' He finishes, shaking his index finger at us all, making a point.

'He has threatened to take land every election for the past twenty odd years now. It is of course a political tool he uses to keep the rural folk on his side. It is a huge concern.' I lean forward, a frown creasing between my eyes.

'Dad, we do need to vote. The country is already in economic turmoil and for us all to have a decent future and move forward now, we need change.' Gary scrapes his chair and leans back.

'Maybe the MDC and Morgan Tsvangarai will be the new kid on the block. It will be interesting.' I stack the plates as Maggie with a wicked gleam in her eye comes waltzing through the door.

'What do you think, Maggie?' I hold my hand, palm open towards her. (This is the MDC party sign. 'Chinge... chinge (change), hey?' I chorus cheerfully. What will happen to Mugabe this year?' I laugh with her as she shakes her head showing pink gums and a row of pearly whites. Collecting the plates up, she struts like the mother hen that she is, off to the kitchen. Her blue gingham uniform swishes around her slender legs and her black tommy tackies (trainers) plop noisily on the tiled floor.

'Chinge chinge will come soon,' she sings merrily and we can hear the sound of water tinkling into the sink. 'Mugabe, huh,' she snorts derisively, 'he is madallah (old) now and he must go. He lives in a big house and he flies to London to do his shopping. The people of Zimbabwe want someone new. We want change now.'

The thought of positive things happening in the country and the thought of a new kid on the block fills us with joy, and laughter vibrates around the room. The afternoon sun streams in through the dining room windows, pooling on the old mat where Toffee and Beano (our two boxer/cross bitches) are curled up together, jealously guarding their patch of warmth.

A few days later Gary confers with Hussan the foreman. Gary wonders if the labour would like to go up to the next door farm and vote in the referendum. The foreman calls a meeting for the following afternoon. There is a full turn out, save a few and a festive feeling fills the air. These guys stand, dark faces gleaming in the afternoon heat, feet shuffling in the sand as they listen. Hussan (the foreman) explains in rapid shona (the native language), what the referendum is all about. There is a positive energy in the air, and as the dust swirls around I nudge Gary.

'Winds of change, can you feel it?' I turn back to watch the crowd. There has been silence, save for Hussan's gravelly voice.

'Chinge chinge.' They chorus as one, all holding their hands high, palms forward and the hair on the nape of my neck prickles as I listen to the deep voices chanting. I turn to Gary and he is watching them, a look of happiness across his features, lifting his mouth and making him smile. The bright afternoon sunshine is warm and the breeze rustles in the trees, lifting leaves and cooling the air. The atmosphere is relaxed and I watch these people, who have so little, thinking of their future. Hope is in the air.

'Well, that leaves me in no doubt about what they think of the present Government, Jen, and they can borrow the tractor and trailer with pleasure. The more crosses for a no vote against Mugabe, the better.' He grins.

'Not everyone thinks this is a good idea, Gary.' I nudge him. I watch as Jarent (a tractor driver who has worked with us for a good ten years) slithers out from the crowd, disappearing around the corner. The agitated shaking of his woolly head leaves me in no doubt that he is not partial to putting a 'no' vote onto his ballot paper. Four youngsters, eyes on the ground slide after him.

'Well, the majority of them will go, and that is what voting is all about.' He nods at me, poking me gently in the ribs with his elbow settling my fears. Walking over to Hussan, whose large grey steel

16

wool beard hangs like a trophy down onto his blue overall clad chest, I see Gary lifting his shoulders and Hussan nods. His bald pate gleams with perspiration.

The following weekend arrives and Mikaela and Ben are both home. Ben is out early romancing the wind, and chasing the clouds; a freedom that comes with riding a motor bike. He stalks in through the back door with a cocky assurance, tanned arms swinging loosely by his sides. His stocky body is lean and well defined; a natural sportsman. A small chip on the front tooth gives his snowy smile character. His green eyes are brimming with health and he looks as mischievous as a leprechaun. He stops, thrusting his chin out and narrowing his eyes. Dancing forward and retreating, he watches me. I crouch, hands on knees, swaying from side to side, my eyes never leaving him as I try to second guess his move. I know this look in his eye. He charges and I am not slick enough. Maggie shrieks with mirth as Ben pops an arm around my shoulder and mock wrestles me until I have one knee on the kitchen floor, rendered helpless and weak with laughter. I slap wildly, as his bicep bulges.

'Help me, Maggie, he is a bully.' I squeal and Ben tightens his grip. The two boxer bitches join in the fun, barking and lolloping around the kitchen. 'Maggie,' I squeal again, laughing and trying to swot Ben with my free arm.

'Get out of here, Ben. Out, out you go.' Maggie swishes the kitchen towel, flicking it at him and stinging him on the back, which makes him laugh even louder. 'Ben, you must not be like a tsotsi (hoody). Come now, you leave your mum alone.'

Gary strides into the kitchen and stands with his hands resting on his hips, watching us with quiet amusement twitching his lips, but not coming to my aid. 'Hey you two, come on now. Let's go. Ben, are you and Mikaela going to take the motor bike?' Her blonde head, as if on cue appears around the door.

'Did I hear my name?' Her large mouth is stretched with a wide smile. A smile that is as warm and inviting as the midday sun. I peer up at her from under Ben's arm pit, my nose twitching from the strong odour that teenage boys wear. 'You okay there, Mum?' I wrinkle my nose and she giggles. 'Deodorant or sweat smell, Mum?'

'Help me, Mikaela; it is not a deo smell!' I squawk like a rooster about to lose its head, as Ben squeezes tighter. She bursts out laughing; a tinkling clear sound of joy. Ben releases me, sniffing under his arm.

'Mum that is a deo smell.' He is indignant as I block my nose and swishing a hand backwards and forwards. 'Hey, Mum careful otherwise I will give you a pit stop.' He chuckles. Our moment of horseplay is done.

Mikaela wipes her hands down her Jodhpur clad legs declaring, 'I will bath or swim when we get back.' She pulls the long blue tee shirt down over her bum. 'Gran and Pa have arrived, Mum.' We are now ready to go and vote.

Mikaela climbs on the motor bike behind Ben, and the freedom of the moment takes them as they roar out of the gate in the security fence that surrounds the farm house. Bouncing over the corrugations that mar the steep dirt road, they lead the way to the next door farm where we will place our votes. We follow behind in the truck with dad sitting in the front with Gary, and mum and I chatter excitedly in the back. The front windows are open and the fresh breeze whistles a cheerful tune as it caresses and ruffles dad's grey hair. The tractor and trailer left an hour earlier with all the labour who wants to cast a vote. We reach the next door farm, where we register our names, enter the booth and pop our cross on the form. We know there is going to be change; we just did not know how big the crash would be. Jarent is conspicuous by his absence.

Mugabe is a clever man. He is testing the waters with this referendum to see which way the people will vote. He is aware of his declining popularity and holds onto power with the stealth and strength of a giant tarantula. For twenty odd years now we have been paralyzed with fear and very aware of Mugabe's ability to inflict fatal bites with his venomous fangs.

'Maggie, he has lost the referendum.' A day or so later, I bounce through to the kitchen. 'I think that he will lose this election.' She grins and so do I. 'Goodnight, I will see you in the morning.' She waves merrily. We have, however underestimated Mugabe's spite. We pour ourselves a drink, and sit back, ready to celebrate his defeat.

'This is the first time in all the years of him being in power that he has lost a vote,' Gary beams as he pours himself another generous whiskey, dropping in a couple of ice cubes and licking his finger after stirring them around the glass. 'Oh this victory is sweet. My whiskey hasn't taste...'

'Shush, Gary,' I cut him off, leaning forward as I turn the sound up on the television as Mugabe's dark angry eyes appear to focus on me. 'Look at his face,' I whisper. 'He is livid, Gary. Check his eyes. Talk about fire in his eyes. Oh my word, he looks like he is spoiling for a fight.' Mugabe's mouth is a gash across his face, disapproving and angry. 'The devil reincarnated.' The force of his hatred is powerful and I sink back into the pale green armchair, rocking gently back and forth, my eyes not leaving the television screen.

We watch as Mugabe addresses the nation, his voice as silky as the thread he is spinning. I sit spellbound, at his farcical

19

graciousness on losing. His clenched bony fist is held high as he accepts defeat, clutching at the air.

'He is saying the right things, Gary, but ... I am not sure.' I watch his 'black power salute', and turn to Gary. He is as absorbed as I have been and as he shivers, I know that he is feeling like me. A cob web floats in the air, stirred by the faint and clammy breeze I can feel coming through the veranda door; a slight whoosh of air with under currents of something evil.

Chapter 4

THE THIRD CHIMURENGA

Within days of Mugabe's speech, the first farmer's and their labour forces in the country are to feel the wrath of this man. Self styled war veterans like knights of darkness swathed in cloaks of violence start arriving onto farms in other districts. Reports over our radio network report on how they are menacing their way to the front gate of the homesteads, armed with sticks, picks, axes and pipes. Wild eyed with alcohol and drug induced anger, their vicious tongues and ready fists are a force to be reckoned with. Work disruptions, the slaughtering of cattle and intimidation in the workers village is rife, as they instil terror into the hearts of all those living in the countryside.

'Maggie, I am frightened of these people. Mugabe has threatened us with very serious violence and all these people that are coming onto the farms will only listen to him. Are you frightened? 'My blue gaze holds her dark brown one. She nods her head but does not speak. 'How does everyone in the workers village feel?' I rest my back up against the kitchen counter, my eyes running around the large brightly coloured kitchen.

'Eish, Miss Jeans, (the name the workers call me, due to the fact I am always wearing jeans.) I am scared because they will take us, and make us vote for ZANU PF. I don't want to vote for Mugabe. His time is past.' Her dark skin is shiny and she wipes an arm over her face. 'But, I think that most people will vote for MDC.' She gives me the open palm salute. 'We want change. This government is finished now.' She takes off, swirling around the kitchen, pink tongue snaking out through her fleshy lips and her thin wrinkly legs pumping like pistons. I stand in awe, as her bust, as large as life, takes on a life of its own, bouncing merrily under her uniform, and punching up towards her chin like a fighter with his fists at the ready.

'Maggie, careful, those big boobs of yours will knock you out.' I wave my hand at her, all the while leaning over with one hand on my knee, breathless with laughter. What would I ever do without her good humour in my life?

'Eish, Miss Jeans, he is finished.' She pants with exertion, and small beads of perspiration pepper her forehead.' She leans over giggling like a small girl, and I start to laugh all over again.

'Maggie.' I smile at her. 'Go on, have a drink of water.' She appears minutes later, having controlled her trembling boobs, tucking them back into their rightful place. 'I think you are getting too mafuta (fat), Maggie.' I tease her.

'Miss Jeans, it is the madalla (old) madam's chickens. They are too good and I eat too much.' She strokes her stomach, licking her lips and making me laugh again.

'I am sure that once the election is finished, then these people on the farms will go back to their tribal lands?' I change the subject. 'I am worried Maggie. We will have to wait and see.' Our moment of shared laughter has done us the world of good. We are just mothers worrying about the future for our families.

'I have my family to feed and our lives are not easy. Miss Jeans, you help me with the bales of clothing you collect for me to sell (second hand cloths that come from OXFAM) and jobs for my children. We have the clinic to go to and the children, they go to the school on that other farm. I have my house and land in the communal land. I don't want these people to come onto this farm. I am scared.' Her working fingers tuck her short curly hair back under her dook (head scarf) and the look in her eyes is as vulnerable as a new born kitten. I stare at her. She wipes her hands and hunches her shoulders and I know that our conversation is finished. I wander back through the airy dining room into the large spacious lounge. The television is burbling away and I turn the volume up. It is all about the Zimbabwe land invasions.

The land invasions are being spearheaded by Chenjerai Hunzvi or Hitler Hunzvi as he likes to be called. He was born in 1949 and joined the struggle against white minority rule at the age of 16. That was when he took on the pseudo name of 'Hitler'. He served as Chairman of the Zimbabwe National Liberation War Veterans Association and organised demonstrations, demanding gratuities and pensions from Mugabe for the 'war veterans' who had fought in the struggle.

Hitler Hunzvi declares, 'we are prepared to fight on.' I shake my head as he continues spitting out his speech, chest heaving with the force of his hate filled vocabulary. My finger is on the control button and I desperately send signals to turn the television off but I am riveted, wishing that he would choke on his own words. 'We are in the second phase of liberation. This is why there is war.' His eyes have a mad satirical glint to them, and his hand movements are jerky. The suit jacket that casually sits on his shoulders shows that he is shopping in expensive places. It appears that Hitler Hunzvi's habits are similar to those of his German name-sake; violence and inflammatory rhetoric are his trademarks. Snapping off the power button on the remote cutting the man off mid sentence, and silence is a welcome solace as it fills the room. However Hitler Hunzvi's presence lingers in the air like a bad smell. I turn and Maggie is standing, hand on her hip shaking her head.

As a farming area, we have set up a security radio network and every farmer has open communications within the district. A rota has been drawn up and every woman in the district does a four hour stint of manning the radio, covering from six in the morning until evening. Her radio call name is 'Hyacinth', a popular choice as we all watch and get light relief from the BBC sitcom 'Keeping up Appearances'. If there is a distress call from a fellow farmer and Hyacinth cannot deal with the problem, she can then call on the 'Godfather'. The godfather duty is also done on a rota basis. The district has also formed what is called a task force, which comprises of a group of farmers who will react on behalf of anyone in distress, arriving on the scene and negotiating with the war veterans. We have a roll call every evening and each family in the district will answer their call sign. The godfather will also give a report of the day's events. We know that it is inevitable that farms in our district will be invaded by the war veterans, and we feel organised and ready for them.

'Let us work like a flock of geese, and if we fly in V formation, we will all be okay. We will survive these invasions.' One of our Hyacinths on duty then proceeds to read out a beautiful poem on geese flying in V formation, her voice loud and clear over the radio, encouraging us all to stick together and work as one. It is necessary for our survival.

The long awaited radio call eventually comes. A young couple, not far from us are the first farm to be invaded.

'Gary, Squack and Suzie have war veterans at their gate. They arrived about an hour ago.' I pounce on him as he strides through the back door, grabbing his arm and shaking it. My voice is breathless as I relay the latest news. I propel him out through the lounge and onto the veranda steps so that I can watch up the road. These young people live about ten kilometres from us. My eyes rove around the huge garden, taking in the lush beauty of flowerbeds that weave under the huge trees, a colour wheel of blooms in varying sizes swaying on long emerald stems, straining to find the dappled sunlight. Borders of snow white alyssum peek through taller daisies, their white blooms breathing in the fresh afternoon air, appearing to hum as the small midges hover above. On gilt edged wings, butterflies flutter along, caressing the plants in passing and at times appearing to float in the afternoon sun. My eyes trail along the tall agapanthus plants as they appear to tower over the beds casting long shadows; regal in their purple crowns. The beautifully kept lawn and snipped edges sweep into and disappear through the archways, leading into secret places and sweet smelling jasmine. This tranquil setting with its plants, vocal birdlife and various insects is our home and it is being threatened. For a few seconds, I have been entranced by the beauty before me, forgetting the troubles in our country side, but not for long. Is all this beauty at stake?

My eyes are soon drawn back to the road. 'What is going to come down that steep hill?'

'I have heard, Jen. Come on back inside. You must stop watching up the road.' He pulls me out of my reverie and into his arms, hugging me tightly. 'It will not do you any good. Anyway, all I know is that if one of these so called war veterans step foot on this farm, I will have them thrown off. We offered our farm to government. They did not want it and now they think that they can just come and take it.' His voice is low and steely. He lifts his eyebrows, opening his eyes wide and flaring his nostrils.

'Gary, you look like a wild stallion.' I laugh. 'I know we had to offer the farm to the government before we could purchase it. I think it is lucky that we have the 'certificate of no interest' from the government, and I am sure that our farm will not be invaded.' I put my hands behind my back, crossing my fingers and pulling my ring finger over the other two for extra luck. 'You sound so aggressive hon. Hey come on.' I pull a fish face at him, making him laugh. However, under the laughter, a grave concern for our farming career blankets him, stifling thoughts about the future. The days continue to pass amidst more radio calls for help and more farm invasions in our area, and also in other districts.

'Maggie, more farms in the district have now got these war veterans.' I am talking to her back. 'Arizona farm now has war veterans, and that is not far from here. I don't think that we will have a problem because the government did not want our farm.' Arizona farm belongs to Dave and Maria Stevens.

She switches around to face me, narrowing her dark eyes, and wiping her hands down the front of her gingham apron. 'Oh, Miss Jeans, why are they doing this? The people, we just need to work. Adam, he is scared because he is from Malawi. They were saying in the workers village that these people get angry if you are not Zimbabwean.' She has also heard of the disruptions that follow in the wake of these war vets or farm invaders. She can also hear what goes on over the open radio system in the district.

'Maggie, we will be okay. You and me, we will get madalla (old) and die here on the farm. We will be two wrinkled old women with grey hair who sit in the sunshine wasting time and talking about grandchildren.' I tease her as I stand stirring my tea, watching the small whirlpool forming. 'Storm in a tea cup,' I feel a shiver slither down my spine; cold and menacing. Turning away I go back down to the lounge opening the huge Oregon pine doors that lead out onto the veranda, enjoying the cool breeze as it lifts my hair and also my spirits. I stare up the road, watching for war veterans. They are hiding out there somewhere. They are invading our lives and breathing fire into my dreams and turning them into nightmares. Not enough sleep is making me edgy.

Ben has been training hard for his school rugby tour to South Africa and he is rippling with excitement. We are coming to the end of what had been a year of intense fund raising for the tour and soon the boys will board the school bus and be on their way. We have spent many evenings in deep discussion on whether we should be going on this tour with the boys. As the day for them leaving looms closer, the changing political landscape in the district is worrying. We are all beginning to feel as if we are balancing on the edge of a rugged precipice; one push too many and we will plunge over the edge. Many more farms have been invaded over the last weeks, bringing unwanted turbulence with them. Anxious voices calling for help over the radio; the verbal cries from desperate and scared friends, prisoners in their own homes. Our district and others in the country are fast becoming playgrounds for the devil. We finally decide that my folks (who live on the farm) are too vulnerable to be left coping with whatever situation could arise. Our friend, whose son is also in the rugby team, will be accompanying the boys and for some unknown reason this makes me feel better. We drop Ben off, and after hugging him goodbye I watch as he disappears with a cocky stride, young, confident and just beginning to taste life.

'Oh, Gary, I have the strangest and most awful feeling that when we next see Ben, our lives will have changed.' Gary leans over, patting my shoulder, 'Jen, there is a dark cloud hanging over the farm and in fact, the whole country. Hussan (the foreman) is also feeling uneasy. He was saying that the labour is nervous. They don't like the talk of farm invasions, it makes them edgy. Their lives are hard enough without the added stress of violent government lackeys pushing them around. They are caught between us and the government. Relax Jen. We will take and cope with whatever comes. Just relax. We need to be calm.'

We pull up at the front of the farm house security fence, and Adam greets us before opening the gate. We thank him and drive through parking the green twin cab at the back of the house, Adam and the dogs come jogging up behind us.

'There were people walking past here this afternoon. I do not know them. There were four madoda (men) and three women' He pulls out a small piece of newsprint and with deft fingers rolls himself a cigarette. Dragging the smoke deep into his lungs, he coughs banging his chest hard with a hand, before turning back to Gary. The strong smell of tobacco wafts in the breeze, and I lift my head, breathing deeply.

The wrinkles corrugate and roll across Gary's forehead. He chews thoughtfully on his top lip. Worry is a constant companion. 'What did they want, Adam?'

'I don't know. They just walk past, not talking. I greet them. They do not greet me.' He says. His medium frame is covered in green overalls, but due to the heat he has taken his arms out of the sleeves and tied those around his waist. His bare shoulders and arms have muscles already knotted from working with a badza (hoe) all day, and his dark skin gleams with sweat. He pushes his floppy hat to the back of his head revealing a pleasant face, wrinkled with smile lines and dark curly fuzz covers his square chin. He stamps his feet which are clad in heavy black gum boots against the rock, dislodging the clumps of mud from underneath. 'These people, they did not speak to anyone. Maybe they are looking for land.' He shrugs.

'Which way did they walk, Adam?' Gary sounds tense watching as Adam points in the direction that leads past the small dam. Gary's frown deepens, 'thank you, Adam.' He steps towards me and I can feel his warm breath on my damp neck. 'Hey, Jen, I don't know. I hope they aren't looking to peg out plots in our lands.'

'There is a feeling of expectancy, Gary,' I mutter quietly. 'I am waiting. The whole country seems to be waiting, but we are not sure what we are waiting for.' I thank God that we have Adam and Maggie working for us. Over the years, we have come to trust each other and they are always willing to give me information, normally voiced over weeding the garden or planting. Maggie and I always talk openly in the kitchen. Gary has managed to quell many incidents over the years due to information I have received from these two employees. I am feeling vulnerable with all this space around me. Our neighbours seem to live way over the horizon and definitely out of earshot. The space that has always been so much a part of our freedom is fast becoming my nemesis.

Mikaela is doing a secretarial course in Harare. A couple of months down the line, she is happy and enjoying her new found freedom. She comes home most weekends.

We decide that the house seems forlorn without Ben, and so I strip off, immersing my brown body in a steaming bath. Never one for lounging, I pick up the sponge and cake of soap. After plastering myself with body cream I pull on a clean pair of jeans and a white collared top, smarting as I look in the mirror. I see as a few signs of middle age spread, spilling like overdone muffin tops over the belt of my jeans.

The sun is hanging low in the sky by the time we leave the farm. Parking in our normal spot under a large knobbly msasa tree at the back entrance to the club, I grab my bag and with a delicious smell from the kitchen pulling us forward, we climb the steps. David and Diverson are both looking smart in their stiff white longs and collared shirts. Both are employed by the district to look after the club. Raising a hand in greeting, they both smile in unison laughing when I indicate that the supper smells excellent. Stepping through the kitchen door, the delicious spicy odour of lasagne and cooked cheese seeps out the hot oven, and I feel my stomach growl. We traipse through the large hall, our footsteps softly echoing, and in through the iron grill that covers the opening to the bar.

I peer through the grey smoky haze that hangs, like a heavy curtain over the bar, swirling lazily with the whoosh of air movement from the ceiling fan. The strong pungent smell of cigarettes lingers amongst the shambolic array of half full glasses and empty bottles that litter the surface of the thick wooden bar counter. We join the throng of farmers, strong men whose sun browned faces are furrowed with stress lines, and the wary expression in their eyes links them all together against the common enemy; land invasions. We greet everyone with a cheerful grin and order a round of drinks and one for ourselves. The men huddle together, drooped shoulders touching and deep in conversation with the odd voice raised in anger about the current situation in the country. The tension in the room is palpable. Anger and fear is rippling through all of us, and the feeling in the bar is one of expectancy. I fight my way through to where the ladies are perched, leaning against the rough textured woven grass backs of their bar stools. Joining them, we all lift our glasses and with each sip, the troubles in the country drift further and further away. The talk is all about the current situation.

'Did anyone watch the news last night? That peace march in Harare turned into an absolute nightmare as the riot police launched into an unprovoked attack on those people marching. They were clubbing the protesters with batons, and using tear gas.' Maria tosses her glorious rich hair back over her slender shoulder, frowning as she recalls what she had seen. Her dark eyes, which normally flash and ooze sex appeal, are now reflecting the pain and suffering seen on the faces of the people on the march. Maria is of Swedish/Spanish origin. She has been in the area for roughly fifteen years now. The clear-cut jaw lines, a foundation for a strong face. Chestnut eyebrows highlight her emotions as they dance to a random beat. Maria's hot temperament is toned down with her dazzling smile; she is a beautiful woman. She and her husband Dave are successful farmers in our Macheke/Virginia district.

'I did watch, and I have to say, it made my blood run cold. I just could not believe that we were watching this shit going on in our capital. Those poor people had nowhere to run, many of them with blood streaming down their faces, turning their clothes crimson. They were screaming and running in panic to get away from the police.' I shake my head.

The chatter turns to children and Maria's twins suddenly appear. They are cute and totally different in appearance. Like little brown limpets they each hang onto one of her tanned legs, swinging and chanting to get her attention. She leans down twirling the fresh young locks and I find solace in watching as their hair slides through her fingers, glistening in the dim lights of the bar. They both stare up at her as she wrinkles her nose, creasing the freckles that are sprinkled like angel dust. She grins at them both.

'Little ruffians. Did Ben get away okay?' she glances at me. I nod. Her elder son Mark has gone on a hockey tour with Watershed College (the same school as Ben attends.) Her daughter Brenda is not far behind the twins. She is a pretty girl, slim in build with dark eyes and healthy shiny hair. She moves with a quiet confidence about her. She gently scoops up the wriggling pair; planting one on each slim hip. With a gentle smile lifting her mouth, she tells them that they are now going to go to sleep in the family land rover. There is a huge age gap between Maria's teenage children and the two little ones. I watch Brenda walk out the bar with the two healthy little boys wriggling, as slippery as two little eels, coiling themselves around her legs and giggling loudly with childish glee. We have all pulled Maria's leg about her 'double trouble' mistake.

Dave is tall with dark brown curly hair. His clean shaven jaw line shows no hint of extra padding as is common with men well into middle age. Dark brooding eyes rove the bar. He moves with loose ease as he saunters over, his long khaki shorts swishing gently as the course material makes contact. He eases a bar stool into place close to Maria and offers us all a drink. Inevitably the talk again turns to politics. Dave is a conservationist, good farmer and always vocal about his political affiliations. Supporting Mugabe is most certainly not on his agenda.

'You know it is amazing how the talk in this bar used to all be about growing tobacco, barn temperatures and grading. Now it is all about bloody self proclaimed war vets, peace marches and politics.' My laughter sounds hollow.

Maria fidgets on her bar stool, easing her buttocks. She stretches out her long sun kissed legs, smoothing the tan coloured tailored shorts with her brown hands and rotating her neat ankles. She bursts out laughing. 'Yenny (because of her accent, she has trouble pronouncing the J) look. You were talking about stress earlier. Well look.' She points towards her feet. 'I am wearing two different shoes. I did not realise.'

I lean over, holding onto the edge of the solid wooden bar counter for balance as I examine the two offending shoes. I feel a gurgle bubbling its way up my throat, and finding nothing to block its path, the laughter explodes like bubbles from an over shaken fizzy drink.

Like a tightening noose the political situation seems to be coiling in on itself, and Mugabe and his self proclaimed army of war veterans are growling with rage. A distant rumbling, like an impending thunder storm echoes in the air.

Chapter 5

THE DAY THAT CHANGED OUR LIVES

15th APRIL 2000

'Jen, I will be at the workshop. I just need to pay the labour. Please man the radio for me. Ask Maggie to shout for me should anyone want to talk to me. Okay?' Shoving the last bit of toast into his mouth, he licks his fingers, gives me a kiss and disappears through the kitchen door. I hear him greet Maggie and her cheerful response, and then I am left alone with the static sounds of the radio network.

It is the morning of the 15th April 2000. I pull up a bar stool and sit eye to eye with the radio. It glares back at me with a menacing expression from the mahogany shelf that has become its home. I sit doodling on a piece of paper, reasoning with myself that the radio is not menacing, just always the bearer of bad news or trouble. Mikaela and her friend are chatting in the bedroom. I have already asked them to turn their music down, and I shake my head, feeling like a bitch, tense and edgy. I had not slept well the night before having counted hundreds of sheep and dug Gary in the ribs because of his loud rasping snore. The eerie 'whoo hoo' call of the owl had also contributed to my lack of sleep. Rubbing a hand over my face, I stretch my feet down, using my toes to tickle Beans and Toffee behind their ears. I am brought back to the present with the radio static and Dave Stevens calling for Hyacinth. He then calls for the godfather.

'Hi, Dave, it's Jenny here. I have just been listening to you talk to Hyacinth. Give me a couple of minutes. I will go and call Gary.' I hang up the radio, and with a heavy feeling in my stomach I run out to the workshop.

'Gary, Dave needs you on the radio.' He pats my dad on the shoulder and turning he strides back through the gate that separates the workshop area from our garden. I jog behind Gary. 'One of the women on his farm has been raped by these farm invaders (war vets.) He has called the police and is waiting for them to arrive.' I do a little side step to get around Beano who is enjoying the shaft of sunlight from the dining room window.

'Hi Dave. It's Gary here.' Gary slides his bum onto the bar stool and I walk back through to the kitchen to make him a cup of tea as Dave relays to Gary what has been happening.

'Gary, the police should be here soon. I will keep you in the loop. The labour force is totally pissed off with these buggers, and now with this woman being raped, you can imagine that they are extremely tense.' Dave signs off with a promise of keeping in touch.

'Someone is going to get killed today.' Gary mutters under his breath.

'What did you say?' He has made my already pounding heart feel as if it is going to rip free of my ribs.

'Sorry, Jen, I am just thinking these awful things and I have this terrible foreboding.' He rubs my arm. 'Take no notice of me.' He disappears again, leaving me chewing on his thoughts.

The next call comes within twenty minutes. 'The police have not arrested the perpetrator, but they are now rounding up the whole of my labour force. They are bloody well going to arrest all the labour.' Dave is incensed with rage. I listen as two fellow farmers, Steve and John (who are members of the task force) tell Dave to sit tight and they will make their way over to Dave's farm and negotiate with the police.

34

The static hiss of the radio and Steve's voice is loud in the quiet of the hall, 'Gary, are you there? Gary.' I take the call telling him that Gary will be here within a few minutes. The first storm clouds break as Gary comes striding through the door.

'Gary, we have just been run off the road by a omnibus carrying around twenty people, the white sedan car that has been spotted in the district over the last week and Dave's land rover, which is also full of people and Dave is in the back. He held up his hands to show us that he has been handcuffed.' Steve's voice sounds distorted and you can hear the wind whistling from his open window as they bump and grind at a high speed, bouncing over the corrugations in the road. 'Gary, can you hear me?'

'Yes, Steve I can hear you. Where are the police? Did you not pass them on your way to Dave's farm?' Gary leans back against the cool wall, placing a hand on his hip, frowning and concentrating as Steve continues on the radio.

'No, we did not pass them. Please, Gary, go and intercept the police. We are now travelling towards the Melrose's farm (farmers in our area), and I would say these guys are headed for Murewa (a small town). You could possibly shepherd them and make sure they come to Murewa.'

'Roger, Steve, I will keep in touch.' He hands me the radio microphone, squeezing my shoulder and smiling at Mikaela, who has now joined me at the radio. He turns and dashes like a man on a mission out through the kitchen. I hear the green Mazda truck growl, idling gently, and then he leaves via the front gate. Dad appears through the door, removing his old hat and running a hand through his course grey hair.

'Where has Gary gone?' He asks.

'He has gone to intercept the police and to try and shepherd them towards Murewa.' I explain about Dave's predicament before turning away and racing out onto the veranda steps. I stand spellbound as the green Mazda truck tears up the road, the guttural spluttering of the diesel engine carrying down on the breeze.

'Oh my word, this is what my uneasy feelings have all been about,' I do not realise that I have spoken out loud until I feel a hand creep into mine. I turn to her, wetting my lips with a tongue that suddenly feels dry and crepe. I pop my arm around Mikaela and propel her back towards the radio, glancing at the clock on the lounge wall. It is one thirty. Gary burbles away to John and Steve over the radio sounding distorted and garbled. Some things are inevitable and inescapable. I phone my mum and ask her to come down and join us in our vigil over the radio.

Mikaela and her friend had decided to bake a cake earlier and they disappear through to the kitchen to ice it. Maggie, dark eyes full of concern, makes endless cups of tea. She stands close behind my shoulder listening to the tragedy that is starting to unfold. Gary reports that he is behind the police and pushing them towards Murewa. We sit, breathless and waiting. Silence, eerie in its denseness hangs motionless in the room.

'Steve, I am off the main street in Murewa and hiding the vehicle behind an anthill. There are a lot of youths on the rampage. I only just managed to get away from them.' Gary's voice is shaking and I frown, listening intently from the safety of our dining room.

'They have taken Dave to the Zexcom building (ZANU PF headquarters).' Steve reports.

'Where are you guys?' Gary asks. 'I have lost the police....'

'Gary, get the hell out of here. We are being chased by the white vehicle. Oh Shit. Go, go quick, Gary where are you? They are shooting at us. We are going to take refuge at the police station.' Steve's voice interrupts; panic so intense, it makes me shiver.

'Shot at!' I explode into my tea and the hot liquid slides down my leg. 'Ouch,' I cry out. 'That is bloody sore,' and grabbing a handful of tissues, I mop up the tea gently, blowing where my skin has turned pink and bubbling with little blisters.

'Who's been shot at? Is dad okay?' Mikaela's wild eyed look and quivering lip belies her normal calm disposition. I put a finger to my lips and hold her close. We continue listening to the conversation taking place over the radio.

'There you go; dad is going to join Steve and John at the police station. They will be fine there.' I turn with a smile, feeling slightly calmer. 'I am sure there is nothing to worry about now.' I am not convinced by my own statement, but I feel Mikaela's arm relax, and I cross my fingers.

The delicious smell of the Victorian sponge cake wafts through from the kitchen, and I notice Beano and Toffee lifting their noses and sniffing the air. Long slimy spittle escapes from Beano's loose pendulous lips and her long pink tongue sneaks out, cleaning away the jelly like drool. I turn my attention away from Beano. 'I wonder why it has gone so quiet. They must all be inside the police station.' For all of us sitting staring at the radio, it is a delicious smell that is totally out of place with the severity of the situation brewing.

The radio has gone quiet. Ominously quiet. Two other fellow farmers, Stu and Ian decide that they will drive through to Murewa to investigate. The relief quells the turbulence in my stomach when Stu tells us, over the radio that Gary and John's vehicles are at the police station. 'See, it is all going to be fine.' I realise that my knuckles are leaning heavily on my mouth, or are it the other way round? I allow my lips to curl up into a small smile, but not for long.

'Oh! No! The tyres on their vehicles have been slashed.' Stu shouts. 'Oh shit, Ian, look. They are coming towards us. There is a mob of them and I think they have come to take us.' Stu's voice is full of panic and muffled, but he is managing to keep his finger down on the microphone. We can hear a scuffle and then a foreboding silence as the radio goes dead.

'Oh, Mum, this is not good. Who the hell has come to take them?' My voice quavers with unshed tears as I grab my mum's hand. I feel as if the lining of my stomach is being peeled away, and with a shout I disappear down the passage to the toilet. My cooked breakfast is kicking me in the belly. I make a vain effort to remain in control of my errant mind. I can hear the static voices burbling over the radio. Leaning over the basin I throw cold water with shaking hands over my face, recoiling in horror at my ghostly pale reflection in the mirror. My skin is as white and lifeless as parchment paper. 'Get a grip,' I lecture myself.

The radio sits in silence. No one wants to block the channel in case Stu needs to call. I tap mum on the shoulder and squeeze past her chair to open a window in the dining room. We need fresh air. The perfumed scent from the moon flower in the garden fills the room making me feel slightly nauseous; it lingers, heavy and oppressive in the room. We sit making eye contact with the radio. It stares back sullenly.

'Come on, somebody, anybody. Please.' I beg the radio. As the warm amber hues of evening start to sink below the trees, the dappled shadows drift into the room, forlorn and still. We wait.

Chapter 6

EVACUATING THE DISTRICT

The radio cackles evilly from its dark corner. Maggie turns and dashes back from where she is disappearing through to the kitchen. A fellow farmer, Andrew calls for attention. He repeats his request a few times, giving people time to get back to their radios. My heart is firmly lodged way up my throat. My wide stare meets my mums and I see my fear reflected in hers.

'I have been in contact with someone in Murewa. I am sorry but he does not know where any of your men folk are. He has however, warned me that these war veterans are out of control. They are planning to invade every farm in the district tonight, and although I don't know exactly how many of them there are, there are enough of them to go around. I am asking you all to pack a bag and evacuate your homes, sooner rather later.' He puts emphasis on this last statement. His voice is calm and reassuring, but we can hear the underlying tension vibrating on the airways.

'How can we leave?' my voice is shaky, and I cough gently trying to control the emotion, swallowing rapidly and wetting my dry lips with a tongue, that feels like a rasp.

'Jen, you need to go and I promise you that I will contact you as soon as we have any news. Just pack a bag and leave the farm...please. Okay.' His sense of urgency galvanises me into action.

'Okay, Andrew. We will pack a bag and leave.' I replace the handset and turn fixing my distressed gaze on my folks. 'Mum, will you go home and pack a bag. We will meet you at your gate.' I am back in control, well some sort of control. 'Mikaela, you girls hurry now. Gather all your bits and pieces.' My eyes meet Maggie's wide stare. Her dark eyes reflect naked pity at our situation, but fear nibbles at her lips, making them tremble. 'Oh, Maggie, I am sorry. I must take the girls off the farm and the madallas (oldies).' The guilt is heavy on my lids, dragging them down and I look at my feet; we are able to leave.

I turn away, swallowing the guilt and tasting the remnants of the antacid tablet that I had sucked on earlier. It is sitting heavily at the back of my throat. I dash into the bedroom. The most important thing is to get these two extremely vulnerable teenage girls and my folks off the farm. The cupboard door creeks as I open it to scan the shelves, looking for clothes to take with me. I rifle through the neat piles, but my brain and hands seem to be disconnected. Leaving a jumbled mess of colourful garments; I slam the door shut with trembling hands. Pressing my fingers against my temples, I massage gently and endeavour to catch my thoughts before running from the room with an old pair of Gary's track suit pants, a clean bra and a tee shirt.

'Where are the car keys and the brief case?' Panic is sitting heavy. I scrabble through the drawers looking for the car keys and also some money.

'I have not seen them, Miss Jeans.'

'Mikaela, come quickly. We need to go. Have you seen the car keys and the brief case? Shit -Shit man, where are they?' I scrabble through draws that have already been searched. 'Come on girls, let's go. We are going to go with the old folks.' I imagine the war veterans, voices snarling are going to come teeming over the hill, like a Zulu Impi on the rampage. 'Please grab my toothbrush,' I shout as I tear the list of district phone numbers off the wall near the radio which sits sullen and silent. Turning the lamp off and leaving the radio to brood quietly with the dark lengthening shadows of late afternoon, panic swoops in faster than a bird of prey, halting me in my tracks. 'Get a grip.' I am muttering, as I run through to the kitchen, a wild eyed look the only expression on my face.

'I hope the boss, he will be okay.' Maggie whispers and I hug her. 'Go quick, I will lock up,' she pushes me away and I point at the cake, which looks so normal in its iced cocoon. She nods, 'thank you.'

The dogs slink onto their beds, stumpy tails tucked well into their backsides. Maggie pushes me away again. 'Go quickly now.' She squats between the two hay stuffed sacks and wraps an arm around each mutt. I run a couple of meters before turning back grabbing onto her hand, squeezing tight and shaking her shoulder, I plead, 'please be very careful, Maggie. I don't know how many people will come tonight but they will be very... angry.' I can't think of another word. Maggie knows; she has been listening to the radio. 'Please tell Hassan to tell the labour that the boss, he is missing, and for everyone to be careful.' My cheeks are damp. Maggie casts a forlorn figure, cloaked in anxiety as she lifts a weary hand waving me away.

'Go quick, Miss Jeans and I will lock the house and feed the dogs. Tomorrow I will telephone you at Miss Sue.' Her voice cracks and I can feel her tension, as taut as a drawn bow.

The girls and I run up the hill to the cottage where my folks live. They are both well into their seventies and looking bewildered. Dad totters up the steps towards their car, struggling with a suitcase and I take a deep breath, calming my mind. I meet him halfway, taking the case.

'Dad, I can't find our car keys. I will drive for you.' He nods his head holding out the keys. 'Climb in girls. Mikaela, please help

Gran there.' Their maid Philly is kicking her heels, looking concerned. The scarf on her head is lopsided, an unusual occurrence for her. She is always immaculately turned out.

'Philly, please feed the dogs and lock the house. Boss Gary is missing.' My voice catches and she comes forward quickly, patting my shoulder gently. 'These war veterans will be coming onto the farm tonight and I don't know how many will come but you need to be very careful.'

'Okay,' her response is quiet and her eyes flitter as nervously as a young deer. 'I will feed the animals.' She turns and shoos her little girl Lulu back towards her house which is up in the corner of the back garden. 'I will lock the gate when you go.' She turns again to watch as Lulu, bounces and skips in the back garden, her small braids standing up on end. The late evening sun reflects off the small colourful bobbles in her hair. She is an innocent child wearing a little pink cotton frock and nothing on her small wide feet as she chases her lengthening shadow, gurgling with pleasure. She is a picture of happiness as she leaps with pent up energy, and unaware of the thunder storm brewing over our farm, Methven.

'Look after Lulu, Philly. Keep her in your house when these people come. Anton (her husband, and the main tractor driver) will be home just now Philly.' I open the car door, climbing in behind the wheel. The car starts first time and the low throb is reassuring. The air is sticky with diesel fumes as I reverse slowly towards and through the gate. Philly's dark face has a greyish tinge. Apprehension hangs off her like a dark impenetrable fog. These poor people have no defence against the mob.

We trundle slowly up the hill. In the rear view mirror, the valley is a deceptive picture of normality. Thin tendrils of blue wispy smoke curl up from the wood fires used for cooking are swallowed into the clouds hanging low over the valley; hungry and black as night. The tension in the air is electrical as we crest the hill. I can imagine Maggie, with her heart in her mouth standing on the veranda, watching us leave.

Over Murewa way, black cumulonimbus clouds tower over the earth, bubbling with malice. Through my open window, the distant thunder roars with rage, and a flash of lightning cleaves the sky. I stare out into the distance wondering where Gary is. He is out there somewhere. My insides heave in tune with the dark tumultuous sky. 'Please don't let it all tumble down on us. Oh dear God, please keep those missing men safe, and please let all the people I have left behind on the farm be safe and my animals.' I mutter.

'Look at that storm, Dad.' I am pointing at the high rise clouds. I realise that he is not listening. The heat and the silence in the car are oppressive as I drive, as if on autopilot away from the farm towards Macheke, where I turn onto the main road for Harare. Everyone is lost in thought. I break the silence, my voice on the edge of a silent scream. 'Mikaela, please phone Sue and let her know that we are on our way.'

We leave the dark, bubbling bank of clouds behind, and the twinkling lights of Harare, like beacons of hope welcome us. We drop Mikaela's friend off and make our way to Sue and her husband Tony's house. Tony must have heard the guttural 'knock knock' of the old diesel Mercedes coming. He is waiting at the open gates as we turn into their driveway, slowly, crunching noisily over the gravel towards Sue, who is standing on the veranda, hands outstretched and palms up. I stop and she wrenches my door open.

'What the bloody hell is going on?' Her eyes are flashing around the car. 'Where is Gary?' and I lose control, sobbing onto her shoulder, as the relief of getting my daughter, her friend and the old folks off the farm fades into insignificance with the fact that we have had to leave Gary behind.

****

'Here we are Sue, early hours of Sunday morning on the 16th April 2000 and now you know what happened yesterday. We still don't know whether Gary, Steve, Stuart and Ian are even alive.' I slip my hand into hers and she leans over switching the TV BBC news channel off.

John had been brought through to the small town of Marondera and is now in hospital with broken ribs and a punctured lung. He has been badly beaten and tragically reports that Dave has been murdered. I push these red images away. A mental picture of two little boys swinging on their mother's legs comes to mind; I feel nauseous. John had not seen Gary or Steve since they were forcibly removed from the Murewa police station at 3.30 pm on the afternoon of the 15th April. My eyes go to the clock that has been in the family for many years. It is now three o'clock in the dying hours of early morning. I sigh as I lean back into the chair and closing my eyes, I pray.

'Please bring him home. I will never dig him in the ribs about his snoring and I will tell him every day how much love him.' I mumble this mantra again and again as the minutes, cruelly crawl by.

The sunlight, welcomed by the early trill of birds worms its way through the windows. I watch the small particles of dust swirl around in the sun light and the curtains waltz gently in the morning breeze.

I sit bolt upright. What is today going to bring?

Chapter 7

RE-UNITED

I have spoken to our friend down in South Africa. He is shocked with the turn of events that have taken place over the past twenty four hours but promises to see Ben, who luckily is staying at a school not far from him. I stare at the clock on the wall. It is ten to eleven in the morning. It has been the longest night filled with Dave's ghost and nightmarish thoughts on Gary and the other men. I sit out on the veranda, gazing distractedly at the lush green lawn. My thoughts, like an uninvited guest hover over the past hours of madness.

The shrill ringing tone of the phone rips through the morning quiet and all hell lets loose as my family descends on the bookcase in the passage. I snap up the phone. My heart is pounding like a runaway horse and my tongue feels glued to the roof of my mouth. Mikaela leans in to listen. I take a deep breath.

'Hello.' I stutter, mouth dry. The receiver slips from my fumbling fingers. Perspiration spikes the hairs on my neck. I lean over fumbling with the receiver, trying to get it to mould to my ear.

'Hi, Jen, it is Lou (one of our farming neighbours) here. I just want to let you know that Gary is okay. He has been trying to get you on the radio,' she pauses, 'Jen, are you there?'

Relief overwhelms me. I nod at the phone and squeak the affirmative. I have tears coursing down my face. 'Lou, is he okay?' I whisper, nodding as my mum pushes a tissue into my hand, 'and the others?'

'Steve is with him but they did not know anything about Stu and Ian having been involved in Murewa as well. Jen, all I know is that they are at one of homesteads in the district. They have been walking for five or six hours. They will make their way over to Stu's Dad where they will be picked up and brought through to the hospital in Marondera. You can meet him there.' I hear the tremor in Lou's voice.

'Thank you Lou. I am so relieved. Thank you so much.' I gently replace the receiver on the hook. My family are all staring at me, expressions full of questions. 'Lou does not know how he is. All she knows is that they will be brought through to Marondera. John Parkin and Jimmy (fellow farmers) are going to go into the district to bring them out.' The relief buckles my knees and I collapse backwards onto the chair. 'There is still no news of Stu and Ian. Gary never saw them at all.' I ache for their families and also for Maria whose loved one has been snatched away with careless abandon.

Sue drives Mikaela, my nephew Rich and me out to Marondera. We make the journey in silence; all lost in the space of thoughts. I have not been able to contact Maggie, and I have left a voice message for our friend in South Africa, so he can tell Ben that his dad is on his way in to the hospital. The phone in the farm house just rings, and I hope that Maggie, along with the rest of the labour have survived the long dark angry night. Dave's murder has left us all in no doubt that these people mean business. The kilometres flash past and my heart starts to hammer as an hour later, Sue indicates and we turn into Borrowdaille Hospital in Marondera.

'Bloody hell Sue, look at all these people. They must be waiting for Gary and Steve to arrive. Oh look there are the Baisleys and Fred.' I am pointing and slowly more familiar faces float into view. 'Sue, can you go and park around the back. We will sneak through the back way.' We drive slowly past a couple of people armed with cameras and note books. 'Oh my word, Sue, look the press are here.' We park and sneak through the back entrance.

'There is George (our doctor).' Sue points to a tall man sporting a long wiry flaming beard. 'Come, Jen.' She holds out her hand and I cling to the long fingers like a limpet, staring wide eyed at the many faces that have turned to look at us. There is a low hum of voices, an uncertain chorus echoing in the corridors of madness. My nephew Richard is standing close to Mikaela, his arm hugging her shoulders protectively. We edge our way through the throng to where George is standing. I feel better knowing that he is here and we stand in his shadow, waiting. I can feel the muscles in my stomach twisting with apprehension. Friends and colleagues from the district pop over to commiserate. The tension in the room is palpable; a numbing sameness consumes us all. We have two young farmers who are still missing.

'They are here.' A voice from somewhere in the throng calls out.

'Move people please. Let's make room for the wheel chairs.' George booms out. I follow closely behind him. My heart is pumping wildly. The crowd parts and there he is. I stand as still as a statue staring, my eyes raking over his beloved face; a face that should be more familiar but it has been battered beyond recognition. I inch forward and he lifts his dark bruised eyes to meet mine; I stare through the dilated dark tunnels of his pupils' right into his weary soul, flinching at the raw pain that glares back at me.

George catches my eye and I stand up, following him as he pushes Gary into a side ward. While George examines him, I escape through to the bathroom where I run a bath of hot water. My stomach is heaving and the acid after taste is bitter in my mouth. We gently ease Gary's bruised and battered body into the bath and he leans back;

closing his tormented eyes and floating. The dried blood from his hair pools out and around his body, a ripple of pale pink and I gag, desperately swallowing the acid that scorches my throat. Few words have passed through his large purple lips and I lean over gently washing his hair and murmuring how much I love him. The trail of red that had been leaking from his ear like a streak of thick paint has been washed away. Suddenly his bruised chest heaves and I reach for the bucket as he sits up retching noisily and I hold the back of his head gently as he vomits, spewing copious amounts of blood. I have avoided making contact with the pulpy mess on his forehead. With George's help, we lay him down on a bed, and I hold his swollen fingers, gently running my thumb up and down the soft side of his wrist, feeling the thick welt scarring the flesh from being tied up. George gives Gary an injection for pain and then he nudges me gently with his elbow and I follow him to the door.

'George, what has happened to his forehead? Is he going to be okay?' My voice sounds thin and reedy.

'You are going to have to take him through to the Avenues clinic in Harare as there are no ambulances. I have spoken to Professor Levy. He will meet you there. Jen, he has serious head injuries and needs to go into the operating theatre.' George passes a weary hand through his red hair, visibly upset. 'I am not happy about the trauma he has sustained to his forehead and Prof Levy is the best.'

'Mum, can I come in?' Mikaela's waxy face peers around the corner and George beckons her with his slim surgeon's hand. Sue and Rich are close on her heels.

The antiseptic hospital smell seeps through my pores, clogging my nasal passages. The metallic taste of blood slides down my throat, and I realise that I have been clamping down on my bottom lip, with jaws that are so tight, they could be frozen. Gary is wheeled away for ex-rays. We wait impatiently, cracking knuckles and whispering. I want him in the Avenues clinic with Prof. Levy. I have checked on Steve. He will be fine.

We bundle Gary onto a mattress in the back of our friend Irene's four by four twin cab. I kneel on the back seat, leaning through the back window and my eyes settle on his face. He drifts in and out of drug induced sleep, tormented by images of the last twenty four hours. Sue and Rich follow closely behind in her vehicle. The shrill sound of my mobile snatches me back from my disjointed wanderings.

'Mum, hi. What's going on?' Ben's voice is choked, trembling across the distance that separates him from us.

'Ben, Dad is with us in the car. We are taking him through to Harare. He is going into surgery as he has head injuries.' My voice catches and I struggle to control my tone. 'He will be fine I promise you.' I cross fingers.

'Mum, please can I speak to him?' I hear the raw emotion.

'He is not awake, Ben. I am sorry. George has given him a sedative. He is groggy but I promise he will be fine.' I feel sick that he is so far away.

'I love you guys. Are you and Mikaela alright?'

'Ben, we are fine my boy. Like you, we are just relieved Dad is ok. He had been walking for five or six hours, but luckily Steve was with him. Steve's injuries are all superficial. They both look an absolute sight though. Yesterday was a frightening day. I am sure you know that Dave has been murdered and Stu and Ian are still out in the bush somewhere.'

'Oh, Mum. I am thinking of you all'.

49

'Ben, you will be home in a few days. I will phone you tonight when we get home. Dad will be going into surgery this afternoon or tonight. I am not sure.' Gary groans loudly, and I tell Ben that I must go. 'I love you my boy.' The line goes dead. I turn to look at Gary, who thrashes wildly, shouting out in desperation. I lean through the back window, taking his hand. He settles again and I look out the window through eyes that are blurred from the madness. The darkness seems to compress down on my mind.

'Is Ben okay, Mum?'

'Worried, Mikaela, and wishing he was here with us all.' Oh, Ben, I am thinking how out on a limb he is.

The press are waiting as we arrive at the Avenues. We avoid them and drive around through the car park to the back of the hospital. Prof. Levy is a welcome figure. He barks out orders and Gary is wheeled away for cat scans, leaving us sitting on a hard wooden bench in the arid emptiness of the hospital corridor. Lonely figures lost in the agony of waiting for a loved one. My thoughts come snarling round me like a pack of hungry wild dogs. The minutes stretch into hours.

'Oh Sue, I hope he is going to be okay.' I stifle the sob that seems to be permanently lodged in my throat. 'Why?' I look at my watch. 'It's already 7.30 pm. Why don't they take him into theatre?' I rub my eyes with hands that stink of disinfectant. 'I wonder how Maria is, Sue. I cannot imagine what she is feeling and going through.'

'I hope to God that Ian and Stu are alive.' Sue voices the thoughts that have been running wild in my mind. Our faces turn expectantly as the rapid thud of footsteps, confident and sure echo down the corridor. I stand as Prof Levy strides towards us; testament towards the fact that old age does not always slow one down.

'Jen, we are going to take him into surgery in the next hour. We have done numerous scans etc. You people must go home now. There is nothing more that you can do. Come back tomorrow morning.' His voice is strong and confident, instilling a sense of warmth into my wintery thoughts. 'I am not sure how long we will be in theatre. There is a lot of work to be done on his forehead.'

'Thank you Prof. Levy.' And he nods briskly, turning away. He is soon engulfed in the yawning gloom of the corridor. 'Well! Let's go home.' I ease the thick ropes of tension that cling with dogged determination to my neck. A migraine has crept up, silent and lethal, and by the time we climb into Sue's car, my head feels as if it is on fire. The roar of thunder expresses the fury of the Gods and I cringe in the front seat, holding my head as the heavens open; stinging nail like rain. Trees explode in clouds of leaf and branches in the car park. We wait while the downpour washes away all the grime that has gathered over the day on Sue's car.

Life will never be the same again. We no longer know where the road is taking us.

Chapter 8

BROKEN HEAD

Stuart and Ian are eventually found under an old man's tangled beard of leaves and scrub. The sky is still as dark as the devil's soul; a perfect back drop for the image of the two battered and bruised bodies being eased into a vehicle. The pain and torture that they have sustained over the past twenty four hours will forever whir in their minds; nightmare spools in blood red. They are brought into the hospital late Sunday afternoon.

'Who are these people? Why would they inflict such damage on these farmers?' I hiss. 'It is such savage behaviour.' My voice is hoarse as I rage at no one in particular. 'I hope everyone on the farm is safe. I wish Maggie would answer the phone.' Mum had been trying her on and off all day.

Monday morning dawns with a clear electric sky. Mikaela and I enter the hospital ward. Gary is lying perfectly still and shrouded in his cocoon of white. His swollen head is covered with bandages framing his discoloured and broken face. I lean forward ignoring the antiseptic assault on my nostrils and place a gentle kiss on his thick and discoloured lips. He flinches and opens his swollen eyes, desperately trying to focus on us both. He looks up at me through blood shot eyes; eyes that have been stained from tears of blood. Mikaela and I stand close to the bed forming a sisterhood; we will not allow this incident to remove a piece of the jigsaw that is our family. Gary's top lids are heavy with the burden of the past weekend's events; closing gently, and we quietly leave the room. In the stark corridor a queue of thirty odd people look up expectantly. Mum, dad and Sue nod at me and go through to the ward. These people are friends and neighbours; all wanting to see him. The nurse on duty shakes her head, bewildered. We are all bewildered.

The farmers and their families are still staying away from their farms due to the invasions that had taken place over the weekend. I have still not heard from Maggie. Our farmers' union has organised for a small plane to fly over the district; an aerial view of the human turbulence below. Dave and Maria's farm, home and workers village has been torched. We have received news that Dave's foreman Julius had also been murdered on Saturday 15th April 2000 and all the labour had run away into the surrounding bush to get away from the fiery echoes of hell. Maggie and Adam occupy my thoughts.

The following morning Gary is wide awake, eyes weary and watchful. Relief washes over me. He is our rock.

'Jen, I believe they have also murdered a farmer down in Matabeleland, Martin Olds. I can't help feeling that this is all part of a government plan. Those guys who took Steve and I were rabid. I have never come across such hatred. It was terrifying.' He flinches and I jump up, picking up a glass of water, handing it to him. This is the first time that he has mentioned his incident. 'Have you heard how Maria is?'

'Gary, I feel sick. They have murdered her husband, their foreman Julius, burnt her home, and also burnt the homes of all the workers.' I take his bruised hand gently massaging over the purple swellings. 'We can assume that they have killed her animals as there is no sign of them. But again, this report has come from the small plane that has been flying over the district. I have heard that she is incredibly brave but also in shock. She has lost everything. My heart aches for her.' I shake my head. 'Martin Olds was shot. I believe about seventy war vets launched a dawn raid on his house. I believe the attack was spearheaded by Comrade Jesus.' I shudder. Comrade

Jesus had played a significant part in the Matabeleland Massacres in the mid 1980's; a ruthless man. 'Martin Olds did not stand a chance, although he kept them out the house for a couple of hours. Gary, I am frightened for all of us. No one is sure exactly why this is happening to us all. I have not heard from Maggie yet.' I take the glass from him and have a slurp of the cool refreshing liquid myself. 'I am so pleased that Ben managed to chat with you. He has been beside himself, and I am so relieved that he will be home day after tomorrow. Are you okay to come home tomorrow? Has Prof. Levy really said you can get the hell out of here?' I smile at him as he nods the affirmative. I know this man better than he knows himself. He has a habit of discharging himself. This time around, I am being as fussy as an old mother hen. He can come home when Prof. Levy gives him the all clear.

Chapter 9

GARY'S NIGHTMARE

Ben is back from his rugby tour. Our world, as Ben had known it has vanished. His green eyes are clouded with concern and after several watery blinks he gently pops his sun browned arm around his dad and rests his head against Gary's. His sun bleached hair, like a thatch of straw atop a healthy brown face rests gently against his dad's swollen and purple face entombed under the discoloured bandage. I swallow deeply as the little scene is poignant. Words are elusive for Ben.

We are living in a vortex of swirling mists of fear. But; Ben's strong presence is comforting. Another mattress has been borrowed in readiness for the temporary dormitory that is set up every evening in the lounge at Sues. We are packed in like sardines and I am grateful that we are all together and safe. The thick burnt smell of roasted coffee swirls through the house as endless friends and family pop in to see how Gary is faring.

Easing my body gently into the steaming water, I lay back closing my eyes. The hot water is relaxing and like a warm breeze it ripples over my body. I am weary tonight and there still has been no contact with Maggie.

'Jen, can I jump in?' Dark inky eyes bore into mine.

'Of course you can.' I sit pulling my knees up so that he can ease his tormented body into the hot water. I sit in silence watching as his body trembles feverishly and his face grimaces in pain. We sit with our knees touching; thankful that we are still together. 'Gary, I am worried about everyone on the farm. When I try phoning, it just rings and rings. Maggie would answer if she could. It is so frustrating.

What about the dogs?' I whisper. The white bandage covering his head is yellowing over the wound on the forehead and I lean towards him outlining his swollen mouth with my finger. 'Shit, Gary. Why?'

'Jen, it is all political. These guys have been given carte blanche to do whatever they bloody feel like, as long as it is for the right party.' He closes his eyes and I know that he is remembering. 'They were savage, Jen.' He shudders and instinctively his hand goes to his forehead and tears slip down his cheeks. I kiss his hand. How dare they do this to him?

'As you know I intercepted the police and begged them to follow the vehicles that had abducted Dave. I travelled behind them, trying to push them to pick up a bit of speed.' His voice trembles. 'There was a charged feeling in Murewa; a sort of explosive atmosphere. You know, Jen, I never did see Dave. Those bastards had taken him to the ZANU PF headquarters. After John and Steve were shot at, they took refuge at the police station and I joined them. We assumed that we would be safe there. You know there was an eerie silence in that police station. They would not look at us and they would not talk to us. They pushed us through to the courtyard and locked the grill behind us.'

Gary. I wish you guys had just driven back along the Murewa road to one of the farms.' I whisper. 'But that is looking back in retrospect. Sorry.'

'I know I could have left, but I could not have left the guys behind. My conscience would not have let me do that. We were hoping that we could negotiate for Dave's release. We did not expect this rabid mob of ZANU PF supporters, Jen. We heard the mob coming; they were chanting 'Pamberi (Up with) ZANU PF' and things began to happen quickly. There were so many of them. It was like a human wave; all screaming for blood and waving their pipes and sticks. It was terrifying, Jen.' He takes a deep breath. 'When the police opened the gate and allowed these people to take us, they bullied us into the back of Dave's land rover and swarmed in after us, suffocating us with their bodies. It was literally minutes before they had stripped me of everything except my shorts and shirt. We assumed that they were taking us back to the headquarters to join Dave, so you can imagine our anxiety when they screeched to a halt and only John was removed and brutally thrown in the dirt. We did not have a chance to speak to him and the door was slammed closed. I will never forget the feeling of panic I had when that door shut.' His eyes have taken on a haunted look. 'I knew that whatever journey they were taking me on, I was not going to come out of it as the same person.' He stares off and a quiet sigh escapes from his bruised and swollen lips. I am mesmerized.

'Breathe out.' I mutter under my breath, exhaling in a loud swoosh. My heart is slamming against my rib cage. I lean over his shoulder and run some more hot water. The tinkle of trickling water fills the silence and gives Gary time to control his rampaging thoughts. 'You don't have to do this Gary.' I fill the hair jug with hot water and let it stream over his bruised shoulders.

'I need to, Jen. I need to share this with you.' He takes a deep breath. 'The nightmare began. They were sitting on us and I could not breathe and, Jen, I cannot get that awful stench of unwashed bodies out of my nostrils. They stank of body odour, booze and cigarettes. They were also drugged up. I just closed my eyes and tried to control the fear. They were screaming for us to go back to Britain, and how I had killed their forefathers and stolen their land. The atmosphere was electrical in that vehicle. I knew that Steve and I were going to take a beating; it was just a question of when and it came sooner than I thought.' Again a silence as he stares off. I sit quietly waiting. 'We hadn't been going for long, Jen and they found Steve's revolver in his shoulder holster. I cringed under the mass of legs as we careered off the road as the driver slammed on the breaks. They dragged Steve out the back of the land rover beating him senseless. I could not see but I could hear him screaming and then I heard a shot. They threw him back into the vehicle. He was so still.' He stops talking, shaking his head; trying to block off the thoughts.

'Oh shit, Gary.' I mutter. I am sitting still, tense and coiled; waiting for him to continue.

'I thought he was dead. I cannot describe the overwhelming panic when I thought that I was now on my own. They wrenched me out of that vehicle and I did not even have time to confront the fear of death. They slammed something into my face. I could not see anything, but I heard a sickening crunch. There was blood pouring down my face and trickling down my body. I could feel it clogging my throat. I don't remember being thrown back into the vehicle, Jen.' I gently squeeze his hands. 'I don't know how much time passed. It all seemed to be dark and shadowy. I must have been drifting in and out of consciousness.' A long pause and heavy silence lies between us. I have tears streaming down my face. I have no idea what is coming.

'The next I remember is being hauled out of the vehicle and having ropes tied to each wrist. I was then frog marched into the bush. The thought that I was going to be executed was foremost in my mind.' He whispers. I sob. I am horrified at the mental picture he is creating.

'They were armed with iron bars and I started to fight because I just could not bear the thought of what was coming. The more I fought, the more they laughed and pulled on the ropes. I did not want to die. I was like a puppet in their hands and unable to defend myself as they beat me with iron bars.' His hand goes up to his forehead. 'I welcomed the darkness, Jen. The rain or the intense pain in my arms woke me up. I don't know how long I had been suspended between the trees. I shouted out for someone to please come and when Steve answered me, the feeling of relief was unbelievable. I was no longer alone. They untied both of us and I welcomed the blackness again.' We run some more hot water into the bath. My head is buzzing.

'Steve woke me up at a later stage and said they had gone. I tried standing but I kept vomiting and everything went black again. I woke later on with the sound of a vehicle. They were back. Steve and I were marched to the vehicle and thrown in the back. It was not the land rover but a white truck with no canopy. We later found out that the truck belonged to Ian, but of course we did not know at this stage that he and Stu were also involved. We were told to lie on our stomachs while they tied my wrists together and also my ankles. They did the same to Steve. The vehicle took off again. The ZANU PF supporters were all sitting on the sides of the truck holding us down with their feet. They were giving us the odd kick but the frenzied attacks from earlier had ceased. I figured that they had not killed us yet and for the first time, survival seemed a reality. I must have passed out again only to wake some time later with a heavy weight being thrown on top of us. It took me a little while before I realised that it was a body; a dead body.' He can't go on. I climb out the bath and fill a plastic mug with cold water, handing it to Gary. He takes a sip, trying to clear his throat. Climbing back into the bath, I swish the warm water over my shoulders trying to warm my shivering insides.

'Animals, Gary.' I hiss.

'No, Jen, animals kill for food. Men kill for no reason. They drove around for what felt like hours with the body bouncing around on top of us. Suddenly we stopped moving. Steve nudged me again, to tell me that they had gone. Thank god it had stopped raining. Steve had been told that they would kill us if we moved, so we lay for what felt like ages, listening. We struggled to heave the body off us and then fought with the knots roping our hands, which were bloody numb and I could not feel my fingers. We huddled in the cab of the truck. We had no car keys and four slashed tyres; our only option was to wait for daybreak, and at least we could get our bearings.

'Where were you?' I ask.

'We were parked on a low level bridge in the communal lands. The river was roaring down and under the bridge. We identified the body as belonging to Dave. I hoped that John had survived. I realised that I had some serious problems with my head as I kept vomiting and feeling dizzy. Steve and I needed all our strength. We had not gone far when I recognised the hills in the distance. It was Koodoo Range (a farm belonging to a farmer in our area) and so we slowly and painfully made our way. We were barefoot and the going was tough. We kept hearing a small plane flying over and we would panic and hide under the bushes. Little did we know that it was a search party and they were looking for us? We had to cross a river. There had been so much rain and that water was storming down. My heart just failed me. We estimated that we had already been walking for a couple of hours and then we had to get through that pounding mud sucking water, Jen, I do not know how we did it. When we crawled out onto the bank on the other side gasping for breath, I remember feeling this incredible strength. I knew then that we would be alright. Up until then I was not sure, but the mind is such a powerful weapon and so we pressed on with renewed spirit.' He sips on the water, staring off into the distance. I am silent. I have accompanied him through every second of this nightmare journey and I am in awe of his guts and strength.

'When we eventually arrived at Koodoo Range, and the security guard told us to be quiet because of the war vets who had arrived the evening before, my heart plumeted. I was devastated after calling for you on the radio to find that we would now have to drive off Koodoo Range. It nearly did my head in.'

'Gary, I am so sorry we had to leave you behind. I can't describe the desolate feeling of leaving something so precious behind. I had to get the girls and the folks off the farm.' My voice is a mere whisper.

'Jen, thank God you guys were not on the farm, and I am assuming that a group of them did arrive. I am so grateful that you all had gone.' His swollen hand gives me a reassuring touch on the shoulder. 'Anyway, I am eternally grateful that John Parkin and Jimmy (fellow farmers) came into the district to take us to the hospital. It was only then that we realised that Stu and Ian were still missing. We had never seen them and had already been removed from the police station by the time they drove through to Murewa. It was also a huge relief to hear that John was okay.' He leans forward resting his head gently on my shoulder.

I climb out the bath and wrap a huge towel around myself. Gary immerses his bruised and battered body in the hot water. I lean against the wall while dark shadowy figures fight through my consciousness. I feel the tension skittering in me as a huge sob escapes up my throat. I know that this version of his journey is an abridged version, a raw explosion of violence and skating over parts that are too painful for the mind to accept. I weep, watching Gary through eyes that are swimming in tears as he wraps a towel around himself. We sit with our backs against the cold wall, holding each other as our tears mingle. We cry for Maria and her family. We cry for democracy. We cry for our country, praying that all is well with Maggie and everybody on the farm.

Chapter 10

MAGGIE

Maggie is never far from my mind. I silently will her to phone. My dreams have been full of smoky images and fleeing shadows, war vets and Maggie; all merging together. What we had perceived to be a real world out there has turned into a mine field. I feel that our new world is going to be one where we will need to tread carefully to avoid being shot down. Leaving Maggie and Adam and their families behind when we evacuated the farm has been causing such a nagging guilt; it plagues me in the dark of the night, a black shadow that also haunts me during the day.

I am sitting out on Sue's veranda enjoying the sun when the call eventually comes. It has been five days. 'Jen, Its Maggie on the phone.'

I snatch the receiver up feeling the familiar rib bashing sensations from my pounding heart. My mouth is so dry that my tongue is cloven to the inner folds of my cheeks. There are so many questions to ask.

'Hello, Maggie. Are you okay?'

'Miss Jeans, it is me Maggie. How is the boss? Is he there?' She talks over me, sounding tentative. 'I am fine.' A small silence ensues. I take a deep breath.

'The boss, Maggie, they hurt him very badly but he will be better soon.' I take a deep breath. 'Are you okay? Is everybody alright, and the dogs?' I feel the blood rushing to my head, making me feel dizzy as I wait for her reply.

'These people, Miss Jeans, they came here on Saturday night. They were drunk and very angry. They beat Hussan, but he will be fine. The driver Gift, he took Hussan to the clinic and he has zhinji (many) bruises. They were angry with him and I think because he is in charge, they want the labour to be frightened. They say that Mr. Stevens and his foreman Julius are dead.' Her voice is quiet and I can feel the strain and the fear coming through the phone.

'Maggie, are you alright. I am sorry they have hurt Hussan. Maggie, Mr. Stevens is dead, and also his foreman Julius. Have they hurt you?' There is a long hush and I wait patiently with trembling hands.

'I am fine. The dogs are fine, Miss Jeans. These people came into the house. I locked the dogs in the laundry. They wanted beer.' She is quiet. 'Hussan is sore but he will be fine. They would not let me come to the house. I was coming out at three in the morning to feed the dogs before these people wake up.' Her breathless answer leaves me speechless.

'Thank you, Maggie.'

'I locked all the bottles from the bar in the bedroom and I have hidden them all in your cupboard. I locked the grill door in the passage and the key is under a pot on the veranda. I told them that you took the key.'

'Maggie, thank you so much.' I repeat, stunned. 'Please be very careful.' I don't know what else to say.

'Miss Jeans, they have told me to phone you to tell you that they are going to burn your house.'

'What!' I spit the word out, reeling back from the phone. 'What. I am sorry, Maggie, did you say they are going to burn my house?'

'Yes.' She replies simply.

'What! Why - why will they do that? Are they there in the house?' The blood is pounding through my veins. I am dumbfounded.

'No, they are waiting for me at the workshop. I don't know why they are saying this. What must I do?' She bursts into tears and a feeling of guilt chokes me, thick and heavy, like fog. I turn to find the family all staring at me. I panic. I don't know what to say to this woman who has taken charge of my home. She is floundering. The silence lingers.

'Maggie,' I take a deep breath, trying to calm my mind. 'Please be careful. I don't want you to get hurt. If they are going to burn my house, I want you to go to your home. Please take my dogs with you, and keep them away from the house. I don't want any of you near the house. I don't want them to burn my dogs. You must also tell Adam to keep away from our house.' I feel wave after wave of emotion rolling down my cheeks. 'If you have to, speak to Jim (the crop guard) and ask him to shoot the dogs, do you understand? I am so sorry, Maggie.' The tension is biting into my neck. Cruel fingers digging into my flesh, stopping the blood flow.

'Miss Jeans, I can hear them shouting. I must go.'

'Maggie, please be very careful. I am so sorry.' I repeat and she cuts the phone leaving me standing with an empty receiver in my hands and the silence pounding in my ears. I lose control, sobbing noisily into my hands. Gary rubs my shoulders, a battered but strong presence. 'Gary I know I sound stupid, but I can hear the fear in her voice and I can smell the fear. I am so scared for her and all the labour. Are there going to be any other casualties?' I blow my nose and bury my head gently on his bruised chest.

'Jen, I will phone the godfather and see if there have been any other threats along this line. Short of going out there, which I most certainly don't want to do, I just don't know what else to suggest.' His hand has gone unconsciously to his forehead, a painful reminder of what these people can do. 'Maggie told you that they were angry that I had gone to help Dave and that is why they are on the farm now.' He is pulling my mobile out of his pocket and searching down our list of phone numbers, he dials the number of one of our fellow farmers. After they have spoken, Gary turns to me. 'There is nothing anyone can do, Jen. We are going to have to wait and see.'

'Gary these people are going to take everything from us if they burn our house.

The rest of the day has me striding up and down the passage, my beating heart bashing away like a bird with broken wings. The nicotine clings at the back of my throat, burning; the cigarettes do nothing to calm my tormented soul, but the smoking does keep my hands busy. I desperately try to keep the charred images of humans and animals out of my mind. The cracks are beginning to appear. My mum and dad pad softly through the house, their shoulders hunched and heavy with the burden of their worries.

Gary and I can't move far from the front door without Mikaela or Ben standing on our shadows. This last week has been traumatic for all of us; we don't know what each new day is going to bring; we are determined to not allow any pieces of our family jigsaw to go awry.

Maggie does not know what the new day will bring for her; and she is living, hemmed in by the turmoil that these people have brought with them. I sit out on Sue's veranda, my legs stretched out in front of me, allowing my thoughts to unravel back over the years. Small dramas had always been a part of my relationship with Maggie, and they have all paled into insignificance with the heavy load she is carrying now. I think back to when she started working for us.

Chapter 11

MAGGIE 1986

Maggie tumbled into our lives in 1986. Mikaela and Ben are small and Maggie and I are young. There is something about Maggie and I instinctively know that our lives will be intricately entwined together; a sisterhood of two totally different cultures and colours.

Maggie, with her huge haunted eyes, eyelids that flutter like wings of a trapped moth and skin pulled tight over her high cheekbones. Her trembling hands are callused and rough from years of endless manual work, and trembling from too much booze. A thumping headache is her constant companion. She always comes to work with eyes that appear to be bleeding as they try to escape from the ten pound hammer bashing her brain. I hold her wrist to control the shaking of her hand as I pop a couple of aspirin into her palm before releasing her. I watch as the small round pills pop up and down with a life of their own before she tosses them into her mouth. Taking a huge sip of water she gags as her little life savers hit the back of her throat, lodging themselves with determination against her tonsils. I leap forward and bang her hard between her shoulder blades; she swallows greedily, shuddering at the bitter taste and gasping for breath. The water escapes from her fleshy lips, dribbling down her chin and seeping into her uniform. I turn away with mixed emotions, feeling sad that this pathetic creature has no self control. I leave her to wallow in self pity waiting for the magic little pills to do their job which, in turn will allow her to get on and do hers.

'I am sick to death of this, Jen.' Gary's frown reflects his irritation. He has just found her leaning over the sink, her chin resting on her trembling hands, eyes closed in defence against the pounding headache. Her dook (head scarf) creeping off a shoulder that is drooping with shame and loneliness.

'Gary, please give her another chance.' I plead, never quite sure why I feel like this. I am confused about my reasoning. She is a drunk and a destroyer of every breakable piece of crockery in my kitchen. 'I know that she is a good person and she is in desperate need of a job. It is her hangovers that get me. I cannot count on one hand the amount of times she has been drunk at work, Gary. She is also as fragile as all the bloody crockery she keeps breaking.'

'One more chance, Jen, and then that is it. The next time she is hanging over the sink nursing a sore head, she will be out of here.' He shakes his index finger before turning away.

A couple of calm weeks ensue and then; disaster as Maggie stumbles blindly into the kitchen. I can hear the water running into the sink. The kettle whistles and soon after she weaves her way through to the lounge with a tray balancing on her one hand, 'hello it's me, I'm here with the tea.' Her voice is slurred and her jaw is slack. With a thick tongue, she tries to repeat her rhyme, losing her way and her balance; she starts to clutch at the air for support. My eyes open wide. I watch with fascination as the teapot starts to slide upsetting the balance on the tray. The load tumbles in slow motion shattering over the cement floor, and she looks up at me with a huge round mouth.

'Oh.' She lists badly trying to focus on her hand, as if trying to find the cause of the accident.

'Maggie, leave it.' I lose my cool, giving her a look that would freeze a mug of hot chocolate. 'I will do it. What the hell are you playing at, Maggie?' I am so angry, I am screeching. 'No, go away. I will do it.' I wave her away as she bends, leaning precariously on the back of my chair. 'You go home. No... Go now.' I dismiss her with my hand, shaking my head at the chaos on the floor. Tea, milk, sugar and broken crockery form a small island surrounded by a pool of reddish brown tannin. The teapot lid survived the crash, remaining intact.

I chase her through to the kitchen, muttering under my breath, and again, I lose control as the water from the sink is overflowing. I stamp my foot in frustration and lift a soggy sock up watching the water drops drip and rippling out over the wet floor.

'She is too much now. I don't know what I am going to do about her.' I clench my teeth tightly. I have pulled the plug, all the while watching the object of my irritation. 'Maggie, what the hell is your problem.' My eyes follow her as she reels sideways like a crab, towards the gate. She loses her dance with gravity, crashing into the wire netting fence and losing a takkie (track shoe) as she falls flat on her face, lying perilously still.

'I hope she hasn't hit her head.' I am muttering, running from the kitchen. 'Maggie,' I am shouting at her, 'are you okay?' She pulls herself up, hands grappling wildly for the fence posts. Her stockings have knotted below her knobbly knees and her thin arms flail madly as she tries to balance herself.

Lifting her head heavenwards, she punches the air with her fist, 'Jesus Christ, why you do this to me?' She continues to curse God and life in a petulant tone; impotent gestures before slumping tiredly like a sack of potatoes.

'Maggie, get up.' I pull on her arms, helping her up.

'I need to sleep.' She slurs drunkenly, and I turn away putting my hand over my mouth, as she weaves off down the path leaving me behind trying to unwrap the secrets of her mind. Adam is peering around the corner with narrowed eyes, shaking his head and sighing loud enough for me to hear.

'My God, she is in a lonely grey place.' I am again talking to myself. 'And she is making me talk to myself, silly women.'

'Madam, please, I am in need of some help.' Adams dark brown eyes plead with me.

'Who doesn't?' I am curt. 'What is the problem, Adam?' I try to soften my tone.

'I have terrible manyoka.' I stand for a second with my brain whirring.

'Yes.'

'What must I do?' I stare at him. There is the huge pile of manure mixed with compost just outside the fence. Surely he knows that he needs to move it with a wheelbarrow. What must he do? Sometimes I realise that I just don't understand these people.

'Adam, just use the wheelbarrow.' I open my hands, throwing them palm upwards, looking irritated. My response to his problem startles him, and he turns away, staring at the scuff marks on his large black gumboot. Turning away, I stroll back to the kitchen. Stepping over the step at the back door, a thought hits me square between the eyes. Damn, I grin. Manyoka is diarrhoea. He is not asking me how to move the manure. No, my mind screeches. I have just told him to go and shit in the wheelbarrow. 'Adam.' I call out and he comes, peering at me carefully from around the corner, keeping his distance.

His eyes are wary as he gives me a baleful look. 'Yes.'

'I am sorry. I did not understand you.' I dash to the cupboard that holds the 'muti' (medicine) and taking out some Imodium, I hand it to him with a wry smile. 'Take two now, and another one later on.' He gives a grin, looking relieved. Our little encounter has lightened my mood. I love living in Africa, and our unique dialogue can only improve given time. Adam takes the water and swallows two of the tablets, thanking me and disappearing back into the garden. I find a dustpan and brush to clean up the mess from Maggie's drunken episode.

This uncontrollable side to Maggie or 'Maggie's dark side' as I call it makes Gary scowl. He strides through the back door as I am emptying the contents of the dustpan into the bin.

'I passed her on the way.' He stares at me.

'I know, Gary. Today is all about her dark side.'

'She is out, Jen. I am speaking to her tomorrow.' He pops the kettle on and opening the cupboard door, he slams it shut again. 'Shit, that is the last of the cups. Stupid women! She has bloody broken the whole lot.'

'You've done it this time Maggie.' I murmur quietly. His humour is restored when I relate my conversation about Adam's manyoka.

'Jen, you are going to be given an English/Shona dictionary for your birthday.' He squeezes out a grin.

The following morning Maggie comes creeping into the kitchen, her tail firmly between her legs. She is sober and suffering. Her floral uniform flaps mournfully around her stork like legs as she skulks around wiping the kitchen counter and laying the table for breakfast. She has found the lost takkie, so both feet are covered. Her white apron ties pull her small waist in accentuating how thin she is. With downcast eyes and a feeling of impending doom she sees to her chores, holding a shaking hand against her delicate head. The frizz of curls escaping the confines of her dook is tinged with a rusty red; a sure sign of a vitamin deficiency. There has been no cheerful greeting.

71

I think she knows that yesterday's behaviour has finally been the final nail in her coffin. Her destination now lies in the hands of God, the very one that she had been cursing yesterday.

Gary stalks in at lunch time. I pass him a sandwich and a mug of tea (as we have no cups left) and we wander through to the lounge, both deep in thought. The sound of laughter tinkles through the open window. Our little kids, their smooth brown legs working like pistons, jump up and down in the puddle of water, sending a muddy spray up and over Adam's gum boots. Ben's small starfish hand reaches out and tugs on Adams' trouser leg, before trying to reach the hose. Adam stands patiently aside as they both tug on the black hose pipe and his deep chuckle resonates, filling the garden with joyful sounds. His medium frame is clad in green overalls and his dark face is hidden by a blue floppy hat; a sharp contrast to the two small sun bleached heads that hover like gadflies in front of him. He takes a minute to roll himself a cigarette using newsprint paper, and we watch as the small orange flame burns its way up the match before he blows it out and drags deeply. He is patience personified when it comes to these children. I lean out of the window, calling the kids for lunch. Adam peers down at his watch, closes the tap and disappears. It is also his lunchtime.

'Well here goes. I am now going to go and have a word with Maggie. Her uncontrollable appetite for booze has been her undoing. She had her chance and blew it... again. She is out and good riddance to her too.' He announces and I once again hear the irritation in his voice. 'As Paul (a friend of ours) would say, her work could be likened to the Bermuda triangle.'

'Maggie,' he calls out as he leaves the room. The phone rings out distracting my thoughts and I push myself up off the comfortable arm chair, and wander through to the passage to pick up the receiver.

'Hi Jen, I really need to speak to Gary,' it is one of Gary's old army friends and I can hear the urgency in his voice.

'Hi, just give me a few seconds and I will call him.' I cradle the receiver shouting for Gary who pops his head around the kitchen door and I beckon him with my arm, mouthing quietly 'it's Mike and he sounds serious.'

'Oh, no. When did this happen?' Gary runs his hand through his hair and closes his eyes as he listens. 'But why did they shoot him?' his fingers press into the pressure points under the charcoal arches of his eyebrows.

'Please keep me in the loop. Thanks for letting me know. You take care.' He leans back against the cream wall breathing slowly, and trying to marshal his thoughts. His eyes are dark pools glistening with unshed tears. 'It's my old friend – he ha….' He trails off.

'What has happened? Who has been shot?' I wait.

'My friend Roy Dabbs has been murdered. It happened yesterday. He was stopped on his way into Gweru (small town in Zimbabwe) by several armed men. They apparently pulled him out of his vehicle and shot him.'

'What. My god that is tragic,' I clasp a hand to my mouth, which is suddenly dry.

'I believe his wife was then taken back to the farm and forced to open the gun cabinet. They took all Roy's weapons. Oh shit, Jen, why. He had only been farming about six months. Why? They are blaming anti-government rebels'. His dark eyes are heavy and I put my arms around him, holding him close, stroking the back of his neck and trying to calm his pounding heart.

'Why?'

'The sons of bitches. Why?' He repeats my question. 'I feel so bereft for Roy's wife.' He looks away and I can feel the quiet as we both stand lost in silence.

'Maggie, please make me a mug of tea,' he calls out, and after a look at me, I nod and he changes the request to two.

Maggie brings through two mugs, placing them with a gentle thud onto the table. A far cry from yesterday's raucous singing. She waits patiently, breathing heavily and fidgeting with birdlike movements tying and untying her apron strings. She stares at us through lack-lustre eyes that are as dull as a cold foggy morning. Gary looks up at her blankly, and I know deep down that she has had another reprieve.

'It's okay Maggie. You can finish with the ironing.' I nudge Gary, but he is far away. Other problems are just too big at the moment and Maggie's drunken behaviour has been put on the back burner.

With our two little chubby angels tucked up in bed, I stand quietly watching the duvet covers rising softly with their breathing. With blonde hair framing their faces like halos and dark lashes resting gently on their cheeks, my heart skips a beat. I feel a flutter of panic, a cold fist in my solar plexus and for a second my chest tightens. The news of Roy's murder has unnerved me. I close the door behind me. We lock the various doors and close all the windows. Sitting on the couch with our shoulders touching, the silence is heavy; both lost in our thoughts about the Dabbs family. My stomach lurches painfully. Are we safe here on the farm, miles from our neighbours? I worry about our kids.

'Gary, I am sorry about your friend. We are now seven years into being Zimbabwe. What do you think is going on now? Why are they murdering these farmers? It makes me feel uneasy, and I know I don't understand the way these politics work, but do you think that the media reports are controlled?' I lean my head on his shoulder, feeling vulnerable.

'Here we are deciding to carve out a career for ourselves in farming in the new Zimbabwe and maybe we should have taken the job offer down in South Africa.' He looks at me. 'No – no, I can't think like that. Zimbabwe is our home Jen. We need to just get on with our lives. There has been no trouble on our side of the country.'

'I know Gary. Our dream is to farm and farm we will do. I just hope that this Government are going to do a good job of running the country.' I wait for a reply.

With the ensuing silence, the ticking of the old clock sounds loud and I shiver. The moonlight peeps through the window, casting eerie shadows across the floor and I get up and close all the curtains. The May night, though chilly suddenly seems disturbingly claustrophobic. I realise that Gary has not heard me. He is deep in thought and I allow him the privacy of his memories. He is grieving his old friend.

I am desperately wondering how the hell I can get Maggie to give up the evil booze problem that has a hold over her. I am worried about the career moves we are making concerning our future. Is Zimbabwe the place we should be? I eventually pull one half of the pillow over my ear, closing out Gary's rasping snores, closing my eyes and drifting off into the turbulent troubles of sleep.

Chapter 12

MAGGIE BACK IN 1987

Maggie's lucky escape from being fired is due to the tragic death of Gary's farming friend. She stumbles through my life on a daily basis, pathetically holding her pounding head. Her dark romance with alcohol is a slow dance of destruction.

Her life is entwined with mine; two women on different ends of the scale trying to get on with living. I don't think she knows the reason behind her keeping her job any more than I know the reason. The farming sector has settled down after last year's problems and there have been no more incidents. We have decided that there is a life for us in Zimbabwe, and we get on with farming.

Adam goes about weaving his magic in the garden; casting a spell with his green fingers. I don my Florence Nightingale uniform, waiting at the back door with aspirin in my hand and a mug of water in the other. With downcast eyes, Maggie thanks me, promising that tomorrow will be different. Her clothes hang off her shrivelled frame, crumpled and worn. A veil of grey covers her face and I wonder if her lips will ever curve up into a smile again. She is a prisoner, bound by the narrow fences of her life. She does very little work and I honestly don't know why I am looking after her like this except I like her.

Towards the end of 1987 Gary employs a new tractor driver. His name is Hussan, a tall powerfully built man with a doe shaped eyes and a gentle nature. High cheekbones appear to have been chiselled by a master craftsman, and Hussan casts a regal figure in his Sunday robe as he glides through the compound, preaching the word of God. He soon becomes the farm pastor.

Maggie has spent just over a year in our employment already, but we remember more of this time than she does. However, suddenly I am noticing a subtle change in her.

'Gary, Maggie has started going to church. I do believe that Hussan might have something to do with that. I don't know but I think she seems slightly happier. I have also noticed that she only takes one aspirin when I offer them to her.' I laugh, suddenly feeling a great weight lifting off my shoulders.

'What do you mean; she only takes one aspirin from you.' He is wearing a funny little grin.

'Busted. Ever since you did not fire her, I have been trying to help her. We talk a lot. She had been drinking that dreadful skokiaan (a lethal home brew) but now she only drinks chibuku (beer). When she slips up, I give her aspirin.' My eyes twinkle at him.

'Well, you know what, Jen. She is a pleasant woman when she is not reeling around like a fish out of water. I have listened to her talking to the dogs and always have a chuckle because she takes your voice off to a tee, and I have often gone through to the kitchen thinking it is you.'

'She also watches out for the kids. I know that is not her job, but she does keep an eye on them.' I squeeze his arm.

'Maybe Hussan fancies her. That would be something. The two of them would make a fine pair; the local drunk and the pastor.' Gary chuckles.

'Don't be mean.' I punch him on the arm. 'Imagine..,' I break off, 'do you really think that he fancies her?' I don't want to get too excited.

During the next year, Maggie only loses her control a couple of times. The pills have become a thing of the past. She appears to be floating on a love cloud, her small bible tucked firmly in the pocket of her gingham uniform. The wrinkled loose skin around her gaunt cheeks begins to fill out like muffins rising, all plump and round. Her dark eyes take on a sparkle as her body begins to fill out the creases in her uniform and her complexion takes on a new lustre. Her sense of humour is bubbling.

'Madam, Hussan has helped me to find Jesus.' the beam on her face is as bright as the moon. 'I am very happy to find him. He, you and Hussan have all helped me.'

'Maggie, I am very happy you have found Jesus.' I smile at her, delighted that she has made her peace with God.

'Hussan has asked me to be his pot wife.' (A pot wife is someone who will do the cooking etc.)

'Oh, Maggie, that is good. You are looking well. I never knew you could be so mafuta (fat). I laugh. 'Me, I think you are smiling a lot.' I lean closer to her. 'Mmmm, Maggie, you are happy? No more skokiaan?' She shakes her head vigorously.

'No, no more witches brew, just Jesus and Hussan. He gave me a chicken.' She announces proudly. 'I cooked it and we shared the dinner.'

'That is good Maggie. So are you going to move into Hussan's hut, or is he going to move in with you?'

'I have already moved to his hut and now I am going to be baptised.' She is proud and I just wish her all the best, knowing that her turbulent years are over, or so I thought! I know her personal possessions do not amount to much; a few clothes, a mat to sleep on and a couple of blankets. Her hard earned cash has all been spent on booze. Her life has been hard. Hussan is a decent man and she is a stubborn survivor. Her new romance with love needs no booze and is adding a glow to her life. She radiates a serene dignity.

'Gary, I knew under that boozy exterior is a good woman.' I am happy. 'Do you know what she told me?'

'What?'

'She said I am known as Miss Jeans.' I chuckle patting my jeans clad leg. 'And this is the reason.' My fingers feel the denim material.

'Ok, so Miss Jeans it is.' He laughs.

Chapter 13

MAGGIE - 2000

After a restless night, my waking thoughts are, again all about Maggie. My fiery dreams had been invaded by the old drunken and disorderly woman careering about the kitchen, breaking cups and ranting loudly. The new Maggie, who eventually broke free from her addiction to alcohol, has been a pillar of strength to me. I trust her with my life. Our home and animals are all now in her care, under her control; a burden which I feel guilty about. Our future is in her hands. The day we evacuated the farm, she had become in my mind a heroine. After our conversation on the phone yesterday, I realise how she has stuck her neck out to make sure that our animals are fed every morning.

Sue taps gently on the door. 'Jen, Maggie is on the phone.' I am airborne; pulling on a pair of Sue's faded old jeans and a white tee shirt. I touch her shoulder with trembling fingers as I brush past making my way to the phone.

'Hello, Maggie. Is everyone alright?' I am breathless with alarm. My thoughts are dark and wretched; choking my mind.

'Hello, Miss Jeans. We are all fine. These people, they have changed their mind about burning your house. I don't know why but yesterday they were very angry. I was very frightened.' I let my breath out with a noisy sigh of relief, falling back onto the wooden dining chair as my knees have lost the will to hold up my rickety legs.

'Maggie I am not going to ask why. The main thing is you are okay.'

'The chef (main man) war vet, he has gone for a week. I am going to ask now if Gift (the driver) can bring your car to Macheke, Miss Jeans.'

I am stunned into silence. This is absolutely not what I expected her to say. 'Maggie, do you think you will be allowed to do that? If you can bring the car, I would like you to bring the brief case, it is under the bed and our car keys are also under the bed.' I turn to look at mum who is tapping my arm. 'The madalla (old) madam is asking for you to please bring her little dogs.' I wish she could bring our dogs too, but that is not possible.

'I will phone you later, Miss Jeans. Today, they are quieter without the chef (main man) so I will go and ask now before they start to drink again.' She snorts derisively and I think that sounds more like the Maggie I know. The line hums quietly and I know she has gone.

Once again the whole family are standing staring at me, questions in their eyes.

'Jen, these guys are playing mind games with us all. But then again, you don't know what goes on in those booze addled brains of theirs. I don't trust them an inch. Don't get your hopes up. We will wait to hear from Maggie.' He shakes his head, 'who would ever have thought that our maid was having to go and ask some arbitrary squatters permission to bring our car, and mums two little dogs off the farm.' He snorts. 'This is just ludicrous.'

The phone call comes again, as promised. We arrange to meet the following morning in Macheke. (The small town that services the Macheke/Virginia population)

Sue, Tony and I set out for Macheke. It feels like a life time ago since I travelled this road. We are driving towards large brooding

81

clouds that billow up and out, pinching the warm morning sun. They are close, threatening and bring back dark memories. The pitter-patter of rain breaks the silence in the car, fast becoming a buzz of angry bees as the heavens open and we all strain to see the road through the swishing windscreen wipers. Dutch Motors (The petrol station) at Macheke eventually comes into sight. Tony indicates and we turn into the garage, the wheels sending up sprays of water as we slush through the rivers of rain water running down the road. Parking under a yellow and white striped canvas awning, he turns off the key. My stomach is churning. The down pour stops as quickly as it started and a beam of sunshine pours through the car windows warming my exterior, but unable to quell the echoes in my head. The world out there is brightened by an iridescent rainbow that arches across the sky and I open the back window and the air is fresh and clean. Suddenly the unmistakeable guttural knocking of the diesel engine can be heard and they cruise around the corner, squeezing into a parking next to us. I fly out the back of the car towards Maggie, who envelopes me in a huge bear hug. Tears fill and spill over.

'Are you sure you are okay?' I stare at her. She looks like Maggie, but there is a touch of sadness; no it is a combined look of sadness and fear weighing her down. She opens the boot. A bulging suitcase sits fore square and it is full of clothes for Gary and me.

'I saw what you took on Saturday. Only one bra and one tracksuit pants. That was not good.' I smile, thanking her for her thoughtfulness. 'How is the boss?' She cocks her head to one side.

'He will be okay Maggie. He has had a big operation on his head. They broke this part of his head.' I run my hand over my forehead. 'How is Hussan?' I ask.

'He will be fine, Miss Jeans. His back is very sore where they beat him with a pipe.' We both stare at each other; we worry about what has happened to the others' man. 'We just need to be careful, as these people get angry and they shout. They have got weapons and others have got pipes and sticks.' Her eyes slip away, avoiding my gaze. We are talking quickly now as a small crowd is building, and we both keep sliding our eyes sideways towards them.

I thank Gift the driver for bringing the car. The briefcase is also in the boot. Clicking the latch open, I take out a wad of money, popping the dirty notes into Maggie's hand, closing her fingers and she nods her thanks. Using the privacy of the boot, she shoves it down the front of her dress, securing the filthy notes under a large flabby breast. I also give some money to Gift. The small crowd of onlookers are viewing the scene with more interest than before, or am I just feeling paranoid? Sue, Tony and I stick out like sore thumbs and I feel vulnerable. Mums two little dogs are sitting quietly on the back seat, tails tucked under their bums. I take Maggie's hand, giving it a squeeze. 'Maggie, I do not know how I can ever thank you.' I feel hot tears brimming and she promises to phone me whenever she can.

'I am still not allowed to go into work, but they are letting me go into the house to feed the dogs. All the horses are out in the fields. Adam is just letting them eat grass and they are drinking from the stream. The house for the madallas is okay. Philly is okay. The deepfreeze is empty. They have taken all the meat.' She now has verbal diarrhoea, giving all the relevant information as quickly as she can. 'I must go now, Miss Jeans.' The crowd grows larger and with a last touch on my shoulder she melts into the sea of dark faces. Tony jumps into my car and Sue and I follow him, driving slowly through the crowd and out onto the main road.

'Sue, what can I say about this woman? She has been amazing.' I stare out the window. 'I just hope to God that she will be left alone. She is vulnerable.' I blow my nose. 'I am in total awe of what she has done for me, my family and my dogs.' I light another cigarette and I can feel it wobbling as my lips take on a life of their own. We finish the journey in silence.

Gary is waiting on the veranda. His bandaged head a beacon, which is why we had decided that he would not make the journey today. Behind him Richard and Ben are standing with an arm around each others' shoulders. I bend over, hands on knees laughing. Their bald heads are pale in contrast to their brown faces; never the less they gleam like well polished tables.

'Mum, we are just showing our support for the old man.' Ben grins, rubbing the top of Gary's head. 'That's the truth, hey, Rich? We can't let him wallow in baldness all on his own. I know he is still wearing the bandage, but that will be coming off tomorrow.' I am thrilled that Ben is teasing him. It makes things more normal? Amazing how we hang onto small normalities. I am so lucky to have all these amazing people around me.

'Mikaela, you did not want to shave off all your hair?' I lean over picking up her long blonde pony tail, letting the silky threads run through my fingers. 'You are not tempted to use the clippers.' I tease.

'Let me think about that one. Mmm...,' she shakes her head, 'no, Mum. I love dad, but will pass on the bald head.'

My mum and dad have battled over the past week. Her blue eyes blur with tears as she spots her two little four legged friends. I leave them to reunite with tears and wagging tails.

Chapter 14

DAVE'S MEMORIAL 26TH APRIL 2000

The 26th April 2000 dawns; a pale pink wash covers Sue's garden in a deathlike hush. The only noise is the quiet moaning of the early morning breeze. I stand watching the end of my cigarette turn red, coughing like a seasoned smoker as the nicotine attacks the back of my throat. The chilly breeze licks my arms, leaving small goose bumps covering me like an unsightly rash. I shiver as small frost-spikes attack my insides; my spirits flag. Today is Dave's memorial. I turn towards the door, wiping away the grit of last night's sleep with an ache in my heart.

Yesterday had been a big day as Gary's bandage was removed, being replaced with a large white dressing over a huge wad of cotton wool. His humour bubbles as the kids pull his leg.

'Hey, dad, have you seen the ice cream from my cone?' Mikaela holds out an empty cone, stifling a giggle.

'Shall we play hunt the ice cream?' Ben cuts in before Gary can answer. 'Oh, look there it is on dad's forehead.' He grins. 'Frozen.'

'Smart arses both of you. At least Rich is keeping his mouth shut. Well, I have now been told by my gorgeous daughter that I have mutated from hunk to skunk.' Gary laughs at her look of remorse. 'Mikaela, I am joking,' he holds her close. 'It is okay. I don't mind being a skunk as long as I don't smell like one.'`

'Dad...' She hugs him. 'Sorry.'

Today is going to be a difficult day, and the kids have given up the teasing, being supportive instead. Gary is smartly dressed in dark grey trousers and a white shirt which we had bought a couple of days before as his one and only suit is still hanging in the wardrobe at home.

Farmers and their wives have trekked from all over the country to pay their respects. Groups of men are looking slightly uncomfortable and restrained in collar and ties, talking in low tones; all wondering what the hell is going on, and is there going to be more violence. The women, dressed for the occasion gather in small groups, looking sombre, shaking their heads and puffing on cigarettes.

Gary's face is pale, eyes drunk with fatigue and deep worry lines erode his cheeks. I take his hand as we walk into the large hall. Mikaela and Ben walk either side of us, strong and protective. The lights in the hall reflect off Gary, Ben and Richards' bald heads, and all three are suddenly self conscious of their clean shiny domes. There are already hundreds of people sitting quietly, facing forward as we make our way to some spare seats that have been kept for us towards the front. One cannot ignore the BBC journalist standing behind the tripod solemnly shooting footage of this tragic occasion. I pluck at imaginary specks of fluff on my black clad legs with shaky fingers. Today brings home the reality of how a life has been taken and others have been irreversibly changed forever.

I glance over to where Maria and her family are sitting. Maria, Mark and Brenda are still in their sorrow; heads bent with the burden of tragedy. Maria looks up, tissue in a hand that is clenched so tight, her white knuckles appear to be breaking through the skin. Her warm brown eyes are stormy and I get a peek into the brutal chaos of her world before her lids, heavy with pain close me out. I have had a glimpse into her moment of experience when she was first told about

Dave's murder and the destruction of her home. I shiver and slide my hand into Gary's. 'We are so lucky.' I murmur.

'What?' Gary whispers, leaning towards me. I can feel his warm breath on my neck. It is comforting.

'I love you.' I reply squeezing his hand and his free one goes up, tentatively exploring along his forehead, and to the ragged scar running behind his one ear.

One of Maria's twins giggle. It is a joyful sound that tinkles innocently in an ocean of tragedy. She looks up, lifting him onto her knee. The twins wriggle around throughout the service, totally unaware of the loss of life and tragedy surrounding their family. At the end of the service a Credence Clear Water Revival song 'Bad Moon Arising' floats around the hall. The humidity in the air is temporarily forgotten as I listen to the music that Dave loved. A few sniffs and gentle coughs carry through with the music. I turn to watch Maria and she sits rigid, hands now clenched by her sides and head slightly tilted as she listens. Her red hair gleams with health as the light bounces off it. She stares straight ahead. Mark sits with his head bowed low. Brenda, eyes red and swollen from weeping dabs at her pale cheek with one hand, and her other arm is coiled protectively around one of the twins, holding him close. The other twin leans forward staring at his mother. He does not understand the emptiness in her eyes. Maria has lost everything in one fatal swoop. The ire of the Government has swept through her life like a tornado, taking her husband, her home and her livelihood away. Thank God she has her children.

'Gary, I hope this is the end of the violence.' I whisper, pleading with the powers to be. I look at the men from our area that had been beaten in the same incident. All their heads are bowed and their eyes closed tight, like men in desperate prayer. I am sure that each and every one of them is giving thanks; this could so easily have been their own memorial service.

After a few drinks with friends, we leave quietly. Farmers from our district have returned to the chaos on their farms after what has become known as the 'fateful Saturday'; the rampant invasion and destruction into our lives. We leave the car park indicating left, away from the road to take us home. Instead we travel in relative silence back to Sue's.

An acrid whiff of danger lingers in the air.

Chapter 15

FINDING THE COURAGE FOR OUR FIRST TRIP HOME

Gary is at his follow up appointment with Professor Levy. Mikaela is back in college at Miss Kassim and Ben is promising to put his head down; he will be writing his O level exams at the end of the year. I look up from the magazine I am reading as Gary climbs into the car. He takes a deep breath and turns to me.

'Jen, Prof Levy has told me I am lucky to be alive, and even luckier to have no brain damage.' He stares off. 'He told me that the five or six inches of rain that we had in the district that night probably saved me from getting an infection in my head. It would have just kept washing away the dirt. He said the Dura (protective membrane) that surrounds the brain had been sliced, less than a millimetre away from total disaster. It just was not my time to go.' He shudders, pushing the palms of his hands together, as if in prayer.

'What? Gary, what about the huge hole in the middle of your forehead?' I lean over pointing to what can only be described as a baby's fontanel on his forehead. It pulses with life.

'He will operate once the wound is healed. I must call him sooner if I have any problems at all.'

'What sort of problems?'

'Dizziness, memory loss or headaches.' My eyes widen. 'Well I could speak to him about you.' He grins at my arched brow. 'Well you do give me headaches.'

'Funny boy, and hopefully I can see him and ask him to fix my headaches caused from your sense of humour.'

'Now listen, Jen. Seriously, he is talking about taking bone from my hip and building up the forehead.' He frowns. 'Bloody hell, I would be happy just leaving it, but he said that I have very little protection on my forehead.' He leans over touching my shoulder. 'Well I am obviously tougher than you thought as I have survived 60 odd blows to the head, neck and shoulders. Well you know I have a cracked skull behind my left ear, ruining the perfect line of my head.' His humour is touching. 'I am still as good looking as ever, even for a skunk, or I will be once Prof. Levy plugs the huge hole in my forehead.'

'When does he want to see you again Gary? Maybe you could ask him about facial reconstruction.' I dodge his playful swipe.

'I have to see him in about six weeks. He has told me I can't take another beating on the head. I told him not to worry because I am getting out my running shoes and no one is going to catch me again.' He laughs. Maybe the Gods heard that smug remark. 'Jen, I think I need to go out to the farm.'

'Well I will be coming with you. You get into trouble when you are on your own.' I pull his leg, but my insides start churning. 'Maggie says those men are still throwing their weight around. Oh shit, Gary, I hope they don't cause any trouble for us.' I light a cigarette and inhale deeply, calming as the smoke swirls around my lungs.

'Jen, we can't run away. We have to confront our fears and we need to go home and face them at some stage. If we don't do it now, how long will we wait? The other farmers are all back home, save a few. I need to go out and check on the crops and the grading etc, and I know you are desperate to see Maggie and Adam, and of course the girls (the dogs). Maggie has been amazing taking on the responsibility

90

of our home and the animals, and Hussan has been running everything else, but we need to go and see them both.'

'I know, you arc right, Gary. Okay, let's beat our chests like gorillas and go and scare these monkeys away, because if I don't go now, I will never go. Those men frighten the hell out of me. I can't imagine our peaceful workshop and home area with so much hatred and violence swirling around. All we can do is hope that they will all bugger off after the elections.' I nod hopefully. 'Our little piece of paradise in Africa doesn't seem so peaceful now.' I smile. 'Excuse the pun.'

'You are excused, Jen. These war vets hate us, but I think they have been indoctrinated more about how they perceive us politically. Let's go back to Sue's and you can phone Maggie. If she answers, you can tell her that we will come out tomorrow.' He starts the car and taking the cigarette from me, he takes a drag before crushing it out in the ashtray. A strong odour of stale cigarettes clings to my clothes. The faint hum of the electric window judders to a halt, allowing the movement of fresh air and the noisy and pulsating deepest Africa to join us in the car. The mixed warmth of wood smoke and fresh fruit flows in on the breeze. I stare out at the garish teeming humanity crowding the pavements; a beautiful canvas of colourful African textiles that does not conceal the crumbling roads, vandalised road signs and the burnt out vehicles. You also cannot help but see the poverty, the stricken faces of children as they hold out their hands begging for aid; thin and dressed in rags. Noisy buses and mini vans full of human cargo race the streets, belching out passengers at every street corner and bus stop. We weave in and out of the traffic, hesitating at the broken stop lights. Gary has to stamp down on the brakes and I am thrown forward like a rag doll as a commuter taxi pulls in front of us, narrowly missing our bumper. The passengers are packed in, and hanging out the windows as the cowboy driver disappears from view with many hand gestures and noisy horn blowing.

'You bloody fool.' I wave my fist at the disappearing commuter taxi. 'Gees, Gary, I don't know that we aren't safer on the farm with the war vets than trying to negotiate through this traffic.' I give a nervous giggle. 'I hope we don't fall into one of the potholes, never to be found again.' They are enormous cavernous holes with rugged edges of broken tar. I wipe my sweaty palms down my jeans. We arrive back at Sue's in time to take a phone call from my brother Ken, who lives in Johannesburg. He has been phoning every couple of days to find out how we all are.

The following morning we are up bright and early. I am a coiled spring; sucking on one cigarette after another like they are providing the very oxygen I need to keep functioning. We wave goodbye to the family and set off for the farm. As we crest the hill and creep downwards into the valley my eyes dart around, looking for hidden dangers. Smoke from the cooking fires rise upwards, wispy thin tendrils reaching to the blue sky and covering the valley with a veil of grey pretence. I open my window, the earthy smell of damp soil and cooking fires invades my senses invoking a strong feeling of emotion in me. This is my home and I am terrified of driving through the gate into my own garden. The deep ugly gash along Gary's forehead is raw and pink and the bruising around his eyes is still purple. All is mending on the exterior but his memories are traumatic.

'You okay?' I raise my eyebrows at him. 'I'm extremely nervous.'

'Mmm... My heart is pounding pretty steadily; Jen and I would be bullshitting if I said I am okay. I feel vulnerable, and especially looking like this.' He runs his fingers over the prominent scar. 'Can you check under the seat and see if my cap is there?'

I lean over scrabbling under the seat. My fingers feel the rough frayed edge of his old green cap with its well worn brim. With a sigh of relief he pops it onto his head, pulling it gently over his forehead, hiding the evidence of what these people have done to him. Adam opens the gate. We drive through and stop. He shuts it behind us and comes to Gary's window.

'Mangwanani.' (Good morning). He greets us both with a smile while his eyes slide furtively over Gary's face and then because he does not want to appear rude, he looks away.

'Hello, Adam. How are you?' Gary cups his hands, one over the other, clapping gently, showing his respect.

He shakes his head slowly, controlling himself. 'I am fine, Boss. These people, they are penga (mad) and very angry. I try to keep away from them. They cause a lot of trouble in the workers village.' He fidgets, stomping his gum boots trying to release imaginary clods of mud from underneath. Gary hands him a couple of cigarettes and he nods his thanks before lighting one up enjoying the bitter taste of nicotine. The dogs are swirling around his legs, and I climb out patting and enjoying the feel of these beloved pets. I look up enquiringly at the din coming from the work shop area. 'It is the war vets, Boss. They are shouting for you. They want to talk to you.'

We drive up past the standard roses that stand like sentries over the driveway from the gate right to the back of the house. They are looking healthy and within a couple of months will be producing blooms that are bigger than side plates. The bright flowers pouring out and over the rocks in the rockery are out of place with the foreboding atmosphere that hangs like a blanket of gloom over the valley.

There they are; a small band of drunk and obnoxious men. The air surrounding them is pulsating with evil; thin fingers reaching out towards us, dragging us over the darkening landscape. Leaning over the gate that separates the garden from the work shop area, claiming it as their own, they shout insults at us as we climb out the car. Maggie has appeared through the door, creeping out onto the back veranda; her body a coiled wire, facial muscles pulled tight, nostrils flaring as if she is in pain. She continues to grimace, shaking her head listening before beckoning me with her hand. My eyes hold Gary's. Leaning in close, I whisper, 'please be careful.'

My stomach is weighed down with apprehension as I watch him straighten his shoulders and trudge across the back garden towards the enemy. The dogs follow me with their tails tucked firmly into their backsides, not making a sound. The atmosphere is electrical. Maggie grabs my arm, 'come inside.' She propels me gently into the kitchen where she pops the kettle on.

'Maggie, I am going to the bathroom.' Cramming my cheek against the burglar bars of the toilet window, I can just glimpse the gate. I grimace as they launch a verbal attack on Gary. The main guy lurches the top half of his body over the gate, his eyes unfocused, waving a weapon in his hand. His eyes are hidden under the shadow of his khaki floppy hat.

'This is now our land. It is not yours.' He looks up snarling. I catch a glimpse of a row of broken discoloured teeth hiding behind the thick purple lips. His pink wet tongue darts in and out like a serpent tasting the air. I shiver, feeling like a silent witness to an ugly scene. Thin ropy arms hang loosely from his ragged shirt and I can see the veins bulging and angry on his neck as he shouts, shaking his fist.

'You people must now leave and go back to Britain.' The other men push forward, holding their fists up in the black power salute. 'Pamberi ZANU PF,' (up with ZANU PF) they chorus, beating the gate with their various weapons of pipes and sticks. Gary is silent. He has not said a word.

'You will listen to us now, and if you don't, we will do a Dave Stevens on you.' They snigger. 'We will take this farm.'

'You have taken the beer and the meat from my house. I do not have any more beer. You have also taken the meat from the madallas (old folks) house. I have not got any meat.' His voice is barely audible.

'You..... Gaarry.' He points the weapon at him. I freeze. 'You will not lie to us now. There is plenty mombes (cattle). We want meat and we are in charge. This farm is now ZANU PF and the people here, they will vote for the party.' The leader is cock sure, intimidating. 'Me' his index finger pokes himself in the chest to add emphasis. 'I know where you were on that Saturday when Stevens was killed.' His insane laugh, as chilling as a hyena's giggle is whipped up and carried with force towards the window where I am hiding, my hands clenched into tight fists. 'MDC supporters will suffer. You, you are MDC.' (The opposition party) He leans forward over the gate, staring with yellow eyes into Gary's, spitting a huge discoloured gob of phlegm which lands close to his feet, and Gary glances down. I can see that his hands are tight fists and his chest is heaving as he sucks in with deep breaths. The gob of phlegm is as disgusting as the scene I am witnessing is unnerving.

'What the hell.' I jump, my heart thundering against my rib cage. I switch around popping my hand over my mouth to stop myself from screaming.

'Miss Jeans, it is okay. I am sorry if I gave you a fright. Come, come away from the window. They will go away just now. Come and have some tea.' She leans over me and gently pulls the window closed. 'Come.' She takes my arm and pushes me out of the bathroom, closing the door; trying to close out the reality of the situation that we all find ourselves in.

'Maggie, are they like that all the time? They are so angry.' My eyes search her face.

'Miss Jeans, they are drunk and they smoke the mbanjie (cannabis).' She propels me towards the lounge, pushing me onto a chair before carrying on. 'These people are not good. They have caused trouble for many people and we are scared of them, but if we listen to them, we will be okay.'

I have had a quick look around the lounge. It feels like a life time ago since I last sat in here. I have noticed all memorabilia has disappeared from the bar. Maggie notices that I am looking.

'Miss Jeans, I took all those things down. I have hidden them at the top of your cupboard. I told them that you had not left a key. I was hiding it under a pot plant on the veranda.' My eyes fill with tears.

'Oh... Maggie.' I just look at this amazing woman, my heart swelling. There is no trace of our Rhodesian memorabilia left in sight.

'They would have been very angry, Miss Jeans with all those things.' She nods her head. 'They are telling me that boss, he killed their forefathers.'

'Oh my God, Maggie, I am so sorry that you have had to be in charge. I want to thank you.' I don't know what else to say.

'Miss Jeans, you have always helped me and I help you.' She retreats towards the kitchen and I sit with tears streaming down my face, thinking of happier days for us, when she had given up the booze and given up on breaking cups. Her life had been a nightmare back then as she fought her demons, and now she is fighting these new demons that threaten her. I have no conception of what it must have been like to have been resident on the farm for the past couple of weeks with these bullies pushing their weight around. We are being shaped by the winds of change and it is these winds that are buffeting me as Gary walks through to the kitchen. I listen as he thanks Maggie for all that she has done for us. I know he is giving her some cash. He comes through, shaken and pale, wiping his sweat drenched brow with the back of his arm.

We sit stiff and unsure, sipping our tea, without tasting it; our home has been invaded and now feels like a threatening stranger. Before there was laughter and now there is fear. The dogs are pressed up against my legs, wet noses kissing the back of my knees. Gary and I are like two people in silent meditation, but in reality we are both lost in the nightmare of what our lives have become.

Gary and Hussan discuss farm issues as I pack up a few more clothes. I join them on the back veranda, greeting him and all the while checking his face for injuries. His one eye is still extremely blood shot, but I don't say anything. I know Gary will have commiserated with him. Hussan leaves via the work shop area and after a last chat with Maggie and loving pats for the dogs, I am about to climb into the car when I become aware of Adam, who is standing close by, patiently waiting.

'Thank you, Adam, we will be home soon.' I tell him.

We leave via the front gate, driving up to the folks' little cottage. We need to make sure that Philly and little Lulu are okay. I climb out the car and her face peers out through the opening in the back door, relaxing as she sees it is me. This in itself tells a story. She is frightened. Her eyes fly towards Gary and he greets her with a smile.

We leave the farm with heavy hearts.

Mum is waiting on Sue's veranda. Her lip wobbles and the emotion is raw and heavy in her voice.

'I am sorry about these tears.' She whispers, wiping her eyes with a soggy tissue. 'I have been beside myself about you both. You seem to have been gone forever.' She trembles in my arms. 'I hate to have to tell you this but there has been another murder. Alan Dunn.'

Gary drops his wallet and small coins bounce, clinking as they scatter over the slate veranda floor. 'Oh shit! When, Mum?' He lights a cigarette with shaking fingers, passing it to me. 'Do you know what happened?'

'Alan was lured out their house and violently attacked by six men.' Her voice quavers as she closes her eyes, shaking her head slowly from side to side. 'He was beaten with chains, sticks and concrete blocks.'

I fight the overpowering feeling of nausea: inhaling deeply on the cigarette, I turn to my mum. 'Oh my god! What about Sherry and her girls?'

'They could hear him screaming as these bloody men beat him. They had to run and hide in a guest house.' Her hand grabs mine and we all three stand, lost for words and deep in thought.

I turn the television on and watch aghast as they show images of Alan lying in hospital. Alan's life has been ripped from him, and the future of his beloved family cruelly scattered in the turmoil of this political storm. I feel such gut wrenching pain and sorrow for Sherry and her girls.

'Oh Gary, this is not going to end is it. They are going to continue to make life impossible. If they are hoping to make us frightened of them, they are bloody succeeding.'

The future seems foggy and unsure. I turn to look at him and he is staring wide eyed at the television, one hand covering his forehead protectively, and the other is feeling along the six inch scar behind his ear. He is totally unaware of me and as he turns; his eyes are raw, pupils dilated and empty.

I wrap my arms around him, all the while thinking of Alan's dear family. I can feel Gary's heart pounding against my chest and I weep, aware of how blessed we are to still have him with us.

He can to a certain extent empathise with what Alan went through; only, as I have already mentioned, he is lucky enough to be alive. Sherry, Kate, Sarah and Emma are never far from my thoughts.

The government's indifference to the attacks on the white farmers and their labour is laconically summed up by Hitler Hunzvi; 'Like any revolution, the path is always bloody, and that is to be expected and hence, nobody should raise their eyebrows at the death of the white farmers.' He smirks. The war veterans are now firmly established on bases throughout the farming community.

The next few weeks pass by with visits back and forth to the farm. The last visit was peaceful; no welcoming committee. Gary is healing and we are deciding that it is time for us to go home. Our heartfelt sympathies go out to another farming family when we hear that John Weeks has died from his injuries after a run in with war vets living on his farm. It is becoming more and more apparent that the invasions and their reign of terror is all a well orchestrated operation to terrorise, cause chaos and garnish votes for a government that is losing popularity. The government, it would appear is going to pick out a prominent farmer from each area, murdering them and causing chaos and fear amongst the community. Farm labourers constitute a large percentage of the population and Mugabe cannot afford for them to vote for the opposition.

We sit and watch Mugabe with his large glasses sitting firmly on his nose , his small 'Hitler' moustache perched on his top lip and his arm raised in its 'black power salute' could almost be described as comical if the situation was not so dire. I watch as he declares that 'whites are enemies of the state' and I feel my gut contracting with fear.

'I want justice for my people, sovereignty for my people and if that is Hitler, then let me be a Hitler tenfold'. He takes great pride in declaring himself to be a 'black Hitler'. With calculated precision he has organised what we call 'organised chaos' country wide leading to violence and bloodshed.

Chapter 16

HOMEWARD BOUND

I wrap my arms around my sister Sue, holding tight. She has been more than an anchor to all of us and I find it difficult to let go. Six weeks of endless hospitality, numerous visits from friends and family and doctors appointments has passed in a flash. It is now time to go home and face the mob.

'Sue, I can't thank you both enough for all that you have done for us. We must go now before we grow cobwebs, or even worse hang around like a bad smell.' I pull her leg. I turn to Josephine (her maid), shaking her hand while I thank her, pressing a few notes into her willing fingers. She bobs up and down cupping her hands, her teeth white and shiny in her pink mouth. There is no need for more than that. She has cheerfully put up with us all.

'Let's roll, Jen.' Gary nudges me. 'Come on, stop procrastinating and let's go home.'

'I feel like I am sending you all back to boarding school.' Sue's eyes are weepy. 'Keep safe and we will come out for a weekend soon.'

I leap out the car, hanging onto her leg. 'Don't let him take me away. I don't want to go.' I weep and wail. Sue swots me on the head. 'No, no Sue.' I burst out laughing, albeit a rather nervous one.

'Go on you fool.' She pushes me away and we smile gently at each other.

'Let's go.' Gary calls.

'That sounds good.' I smile at him. 'Maggie is so looking forward to us getting home. She has given me a list of things we need, so..., yup, I am ready.' I roll down my window blowing kisses to both Sue and Tony, as they stand at the gate, waving us through. We slow down waiting for the old orange Mercedes, which had always been nicknamed 'Greasy dick', for no other reason than it is such a disgusting colour. My folks suddenly seem too small for the car as dad's old farm hat peers at us over the steering wheel. Their two little dogs are bobbing around on the back seat and I can imagine them yapping in excitement.

The countryside speeds by and soon our farm sign comes into view and we are slowing down and turning off onto our private dirt road.

'You ready, Jen?' Gary puts a warm hand on my knee, squeezing gently.

'Gary, I am as ready as I will ever be.' My eyes flicker nervously. 'Hey, who are those people up ahead?' My heart flutters, as I do a silent count. 'There are eight of them, Gary.' I am pointing with my index finger. We keep moving slowly and with a sigh of relief I realise it is a group of women from the workers village. 'Oh!! Gary.' I breathe deeply trying to control my hammering heart.

'Good afternoon', they call out in unison waving their dark arms with abundant merriment as they look past us towards the turn off and see old 'greasy dick' easing up behind us. We have ground to a halt. 'Are you coming back onto the farm now?'

'Good afternoon', we greet them back, 'Yes Mai Peter (Mrs Peter, wife of the head cattleman), we are back.' A couple of them start to wiggle their hips, their colourful skirts swishing a rhythm around their slender legs. Mai Peter who is as plump as a well covered hen, folds her well rounded arms over her ample bust, jiggling rhythmically as puffs of dust rise up, before settling like a sprinkling of brown flour on her wide tacky clad feet. The others watch her, laughing and clapping, then with a whistle and huge grins on their faces, they move aside and wave us through. I crane my neck to wave and watch as my folks are treated to the same merry welcome.

'Oh, Gary, I feel so emotional.' I dab at my eyes with a tissue. 'What a lovely welcome home. I was not sure what to expect.'

'Jen, these people just want peace and harmony as much as we do. I feel for them all as they are more vulnerable than we are. Their only protection is their numbers, but even then I don't believe that they will stand up to these people. These war vets have too much clout and 'The law' behind them.'

We settle the folks into their house. Philly is bobbing around with as much energy as a pup, rushing back and forth from the car carrying cases and bags of groceries. She is wearing a huge grin, happy to have them back. Little Lulu is peeping at us from behind the gnarled old msasa tree in the back garden. I wave and she grins before taking off across the back lawn like a small springbok, leaping with joy, little plaits standing stiffly over her dark head, whistling to the little dogs. We wave goodbye and make our way down the small incline to our own home. Adam's smile spreads across his dark face and lighting up his eyes. He opens the gate. Maggie is waiting on the back veranda. Her smile is genuine and I get a glimpse of pink gums as she strides towards the car, arms swinging loosely at her sides. I peer towards the gate leading towards the workshop. She sees my glance.

'Miss Jeans, they are now living up on the top section. They use the tractor and trailer to come down every morning. Jarent drives them. You will be okay.' She smiles, reassuring me, and we both reach into the boot for the various pieces of luggage that need to go into the house. The smell of wood smoke clings to her clothes. It is the smell of home.

Beano and Toffee's fat rumps curl and roll around our legs, their faces beaming with wide open mouths and panting pink tongues. Their stumpy tails wriggle and twitch with excitement. They instinctively know that we are back. I drop grocery bags on the counter in the kitchen and crouch down stroking them both as they bury their heads into my hair, fleeing me gently. I laugh. It is a joyful tinkle.

Hussan is waiting for Gary at the workshop and I walk through to the lounge where I open the huge Oregon pine doors. I am alone, like the prisoner I am on the huge veranda, staring through the iron bars that have been added for safety.

Drinking in the rich blues, yellows, reds and oranges quivering atop the bright green stems as they pulsate quietly in tune with the evening breeze; I am tempted to unlock the gate and reacquaint myself with this emerald paradise that is my garden. I step out from behind the cage; wriggling my toes and laughing as the small green spikes of grass creep through welcoming me back. The cackle of our pet guinea fowl resonates on the breeze as he greets me with noisy aplomb. I weave through the covered arches, breathing in the sweet smelling jasmine, waving my arms and slapping my palms together around my head as the mosquitoes and midges, like kamikaze pilots bombard my face and ears. Our neighbour, Mark pops around at five to welcome us home. We open a couple of beers, sitting out on the lawn surrounded by the honeyed close of day and the gentle chirp of evening song from the waterway and the various trees in the garden.

As darkness slowly blankets the garden, we lock ourselves into the house, light the wood fire in the lounge and Gary pours us each a drink, dropping in blocks of ice before he hands my glass to me. The room is bathed in a soft orange glow from the open fire as it splutters and spits, belching smoke before settling into a steady crackle. I stand in front of the fireplace fanning the flames with an old newspaper.

The dogs curl up on the small mat taking advantage of the heat radiating out into the room as they pant softly, pink tongues lolling gently up and down. The radio roll call starts at 7.00pm and Gary answers our call '11, we are back.' A welcome cheer comes over the airwaves from the district.

'It is good to be home Jen. I can't wait to get out and about tomorrow.' Gary smiles at me. We sit listening to the familiar crackle and static of the radio, and once the roll call and evening report is finished, we wander through to the kitchen touching things gently with our fingers and deciding what we should do for supper.

The following morning with golden sun rays breaking through the clouds, the bedroom is bathed in delicious warmth. I roll onto my back pulling the duvet over my head. The abrasive crowing of a scrawny necked rooster sets the tone for every other feathered rival in the vicinity. Listening to them vocalising their morning calls, I sit bolt upright, registering that I am home. Swinging my legs over the side of the bed, I slip on my track suit and wander through to the kitchen to make a cup of coffee.

'Morning, Maggie.' I laugh at her delighted expression and gurgle of pure joy. Settling on the veranda steps, the pink dawn throws a tranquil light over the garden. Lazy rays are soon winking at me through the emerald canopies and stroking my bare feet. I stretch my legs out listening to the guttural growl of the tractors as they leave the workshop area, devouring up the kilometres, spluttering and choking in their own dust. The earthy smells and scent of morning is sweet as it drifts in on a light breeze, welcoming me home and enhancing the toasted aroma of my coffee.

The soft clank of the dog dishes and the gentle snarls as they protect their meat and vegetable goulash from the others' prying eyes and chancing tongue makes me laugh. The two boxer bitches join me on the steps. Beano's soft white fur and large brown eyes are her saving grace. Large floppy jowls hang either side of her pushed in nose. Her long pink tongue rolls out, friendly and wet; always on the ready for a loving kiss as she grunts softly to get my attention. I take her ugly head between my hands, gently massaging her floppy ears, and she radiates contentment. Toffee nudges me and I turn, hugging her too. She is a warm brown brindle with short bristly hair. Her long aristocratic nose presses into my hair, warm breath and chilly wet snout leaving damp kisses on my neck. I curl an arm around each of my sentinels drinking in their warm buttery smell of popcorn.

This is my home. I love this farm and everything it has to offer us. Staring up the road, the bush is an array of browns, wheat and golden hues. The breeze rustles noisily, lifting leaves and tossing them in the air before whispering up the valley and snaking through the winter landscape; the voice of the spirits romancing the bush.

A loud shout and angry retort from Gary at the workshop has me leaping to my feet and out of my reverie. Clanging the grill door on the veranda, I lock it and run inside. I am at the kitchen door, looking out anxiously when I see him striding through the back gate, his face as dark as a thundercloud. I realise how vulnerable we are and how quickly our circumstances can change. His expression is a reflection of the turbulent feeling in the air and I dash over to him.

'What on earth was all that shouting, Gary?' I am trotting briskly to keep up with him.

'Jen, not even home one day and the shit has already started. They are just making demands. I know they slaughtered a couple of cows while we were off the farm, but they are demanding another one now. They are also demanding water in a water cart for drinking and, to be honest they are just there, menacing and more lethal than a pack of rabid dogs. They threatened me again.' He takes his cap off. His scar stands out ridged and angry, running up his weathered forehead like a furrow. I avert my eyes.

'Where is dad?'

'He is in the grading shed, Jen. I am downing a cup of tea and then I will go down and see him. You know what he is like. He is not going to stay put at home. It would drive him demented. I suppose I am just trying to get the lay of the land here. Hussan was close by while the entire shouting was taking place. I feel like the new kid on the block. Jen, I have a feeling that this is what our lives have become.'

'No.' I stamp my foot. 'You mean you don't think these people are going to go away?' I look at him as he shakes his head and my stomach lurches. 'Well, what are we going to do then? We are not going to let them just take over our lives and our farm. No, the government did not want the farm. We haven't even finished paying for it yet.'

'I know, but I have a feeling that these people don't give a damn about whether we have finished paying for the farm or not.'

'Gary, just don't lose your temper please.' I take him by the arm as he assures me he would not dare. I look up at Maggie and Adam, who both stand staring at their feet. 'Oh my God, look at

107

those two, Gary. I don't think we know the half of what has been going on over the last six weeks.' I whisper. 'Just keep your temper, Gary.' I repeat myself. Our two domestics look up as we approach. Dejection like invisible bonds, binds us all together and my excitement of being home slithers away without a trace of footprints.

Chapter 17

MAGGIE'S ORDEAL

Our first couple of days back home fly past and we are soon back into a routine, all be it a strange one. Maggie keeps me sane and I help to keep her from falling off the edge of the precipice that we are all teetering on. She is relieved that we are home now as her life has been arduous with the onset of these war veterans. Her humour is bubbling through once again. I have taken to sitting close to the radio, my charcoal or pencil flying over the pages as I sketch until my fingers grow stiff and weary. Maggie folds her arms over her ample boobs, hands gripping onto her elbows and sashays past me, exaggerating the sway of her hips.

'What's up, my busy little girl?' She purses her lips to stop herself from smiling.

'Good morning, Maggie.' I can't stop the burst of laughter at her ridiculous greeting, and this unleashes the show off that she really is.

'Miss Jeans, would you like a cuppa?' She giggles as she has heard me asking Gary this question over the years. 'And what are you having for brekkie?' (Our version of breakfast) bubbles out, as she takes my voice off to a tee. We chuckle; rejuvenating our souls with the powerful weapon of laughter. I take a deep breath and even the air feels cleaner.

'You should have been a doctor, Miss Jeans.' She leans over, picking up the paper where I am sketching a hand, a small frown pulling her course black eyebrows together.

'You think I should have been a doctor Maggie? Why?' I burst out laughing.

'Well, you are very clever and you can draw this hand very well. A doctor knows all about the body, and so do you.' She is so sincere, that I stop laughing.

'Thank you, Maggie, but I don't think I would be a good doctor.' I flash a grin at her.

'Why?'

'Well, mainly because I don't like blood and would probably faint and need a doctor.' And another giggle bursts forth. We both bend over laughing together again, and I inhale the familiar smell of wood smoke that clings to her clothes.

The radio screams at us. The war vets are threatening J.J, a fellow farmer. Like all of us farmers, him and his labour has had no end of troubles and threats. We both look up at each other, laughter quickly being replaced by tension. A smell of decay pervades the room.

'When is this going to stop, Miss Jeans? It is very hard for us in the village. They threaten us all the time. They have beaten a few of the men, but luckily not badly.' She shakes her head. 'Hussan, he says, he does not think that they are going to go away.

The radio interrupts my train of thought. J.J. has to call on the godfather and possibly the task force. 'I don't know what is going to happen to us all Maggie.' I turn the radio down. The predicament we find ourselves in is magnified by the silence. I am lost in thought when Maggie sighs deeply and I look up.

'What's up, Maggie?' Her sad smile hovers.

'These men, they are very cruel. I want to tell you what they did to me.' Her voice trembles. I stare up at her, my eyebrows forming question marks. My heart starts to beat a rapid tattoo against my chest.

'What do you mean, Maggie?' I knew she had been keeping something to herself. 'Did they hurt you?' I can feel my stomach twisting.

'They took me to the dam, Miss Jeans.' I look puzzled. 'They took me and they pushed my head under the water.'

'What!' I interrupt my voice high and squeaky.

'Some of them held my arms and the others pushed me down.' Her voice is guarded and she looks over her shoulder towards the window where the sunny crisp day is laughing at us. I get up, closing the outside world out, and she nods her thanks.

'Maggie. What?' I am stunned. 'Why would they do that to you? I am sorry, but I don't understand.'

'Miss Jeans, me I thought I was going to die. They push and push and I can feel in here.' She rubs her chest, 'it was very painful and I had no more breath. They pull me up and they are laughing, and one he hooks my dook out the water and throws it at me, telling me to wipe my face.' Her eyes are glistening with tears and she wipes them away with the back of her hand. I hand her a tissue. 'They start to push me again, and I take a big breath before the water, it comes over me again.'

'Shit!' I spit it out. I am so angry with these people. How dare they do this?

'Miss Jeans, they pull me out again and throw me on the ground. They are laughing at me. I am trying to breathe. Hussan, he comes running very fast and he is shouting at them, and asking them to please leave me alone. He is telling them that I am his wife, and they all start shouting at Hussan. I run away as I am very scared and then Hussan starts to argue with them. He tells them that he is the pastor and that is when they beat him.' Her shoulders crumble and I am so dumbfounded at what I have heard, I take a second or two to react. I am spitting mad and once she has composed herself, I find I am pacing back and forth along the length of the dining room. The room is cold; a whisper of evil swirls around us both and I can taste it, this bitter poison eroding our lives.

'Maggie, did this happen soon after that weekend?' We all call the fateful weekend 'that' weekend, when our lives stopped being normal. I stare at her as she nods the affirmative. I feel such an overwhelming love and admiration for this woman, trying to get my head around the cruelty bestowed upon her, and she still came in before light to feed my dogs. 'I am so sorry that they did this to you. Bastards.'

'I am lucky because I saw God, but he did not want me yet.'

'Maggie, I am very glad he did not want you yet. We are going to grow old together, here on this farm.' I shake my head. 'Was Jarent there?'

'No.' And I feel relief.

The stark realisation hits me; none of us are of the slightest importance to the powers that be. This government is playing a clever and strategic game of chess with all of us citizens. We are all pawns on this colossal chess board, being pushed from square to square by a king greedy for power; none of us are in control of our lives.

My mind is still connected to a quiet and detached place when Gary comes in at the end of the day. He sits, shaking his head and not a word has passed through his lips as I repeat Maggie's ordeal.

'Bastards.' He spits out when I have finished. 'Jen, these people are vicious and mean. Poor Maggie, I am sorry that she went through that ordeal. We all need to be careful.'

We nudge towards the middle of June 2000.

For weeks now Maggie and Adam have been coming to work in the mornings with bloodshot eyes, exhausted and with spirits flagging. They have been forced to attend 'all night pungwees' (political meetings) where they have been made to sing and dance and pledge their support for the ruling party. They are frightened and dare not disobey for fear of retaliation. The intimidation country wide has been horrendous in the lead up to elections.

Mugabe wins the elections. I burst into tears as I know that we are now running along a different road. The feeling of permanence has become a mere dream. We are nothing more than a fleeting shadow, marking the hands of time.

'Jen, don't cry.' Gary takes me into his arms. We knew that this was going to be the result. 'We are just going to have to carry on farming for as long as possible.' I wrap my arms around his neck, my head on his shoulder as I sob uncontrollably leaving a large dark patch of salty tears as testament to my despair.

Maggie trudges through with drooping shoulders, eyes downcast and a heavy heart.

'Eish.' She shakes her head sadly. 'What are they going to do now? I hope they will leave us alone. They tell us that this is their farm. It does not belong to you. And now they have won the

113

election.' Her hand trembles as it goes to her throat. I know she is disappointed with the result but relieved that the intimidation is over now. Or is it?

I stand out on the veranda watching through the binoculars as Jarent ploughs the land in front of the house. His back is stooped against the boredom of driving the tractor hour after hour and day after day as he has done over the past ten years. His aloof manner does not detract from his driving skills; perfect straight ridges to sow his seeds of discontent. Gary needs to watch this guy. Seventy odd trouble makers on the farm is more than enough for us to handle without having to watch an old trusted employee. My mind churns over, trying to remember the feeling of freedom that this farm had given us before 'that' weekend.

Chapter 18

METHVEN RANCH IS FULL OF UNWANTED WAR VETS
2000

Weeks have passed since the 2000 election results were announced. We wait with bated breath for these unwanted visitors to leave our farm, but they seem to be fast becoming a permanent evil fixture. Dark tales of atrocities used against the labour and their families loom over us all like clouds of despair. It is barbaric. These people are a menacing presence on the land and Gary does well to keep his temper. I no longer venture out of the security fence. No more walking on my beloved farm.

I am once again doing my Hyacinth duties and listening with distress and a heavy heart to the violent man made storms raging through the Zimbabwean countryside. The end of September 2000 is closing in. We have now been living with between seventy and eighty war vets on the farm for months; a hard pill to swallow. One wrong move and we could unleash the beast.

Gary is doing his best to ignore the threats, which are spat like rusty barbs at him on a daily basis. He chooses to get on, as best he can with preparations for the planting of the next tobacco crops. We live our lives on the edge, nervous as hell and never sure what the following day will bring. I am forever folding my arms behind my back and crossing fingers that we will not become casualties. We know of so many people, black and white who have become statistics of the land grab.

Mum and dad have been resident on the farm for a couple of years. This is their retirement plan; everything hangs in the balance for them. We have a new war vet leader on the farm. She is a harridan. Her sneering thin top lip covers the few remaining discoloured teeth that stick out crudely from her pink gums. Her unfathomable eyes, whites yellowed and suggesting a jaundiced liver stare you down. Tight grey curls crown the top of her head and a possible injury from years past dogs her as she limps; possibly in pain which could then account for her mean and aggressive disposition. Her mud hut with its mop of thatch is built within a stone's throw of mum and dad's gate. Her cattle with their long horns and hungry mouths cause many an argument with Gary, as they trample tobacco seed beds and lands full of vegetables for export into Tesco UK. She is like a rusty barb in Gary's side.

'You Geerry, you must leave now. This is my farm, and I do not want you here.' She sneers, hand clenched in the ZANU PF salute.

'I will leave when the Government give me orders to leave, and not you.' He talks through his teeth, a sure sign of anger. 'You will please keep your cattle out of my crops.' And he walks away with the sound of her wild cackling irritating his eardrums. 'Oh shut up you witch.' He mutters under his breath.

She makes mum's hair stand on end as she rattles the gate, ordering Philly around like a personal servant. She shouts and Philly runs. Mum stomps up to the security fence, gnashing her teeth as they meet nose to nose, the diamond mesh her only defence between them.

'Go away. Stop pestering Philly and go and do something useful in the world.' Mum glares at her.

'You, you white bitch, go back to Britain. Go back to Blair.' She cackles. 'You, we do not want you in our country.' She hisses through the fence like an angry black mamba, and just as deadly. 'Me, I am waiting because soon I am going to live in your house.' She points over mum's shoulder towards the back door. 'Yes, white bitch, that is my home and very soon, me, I will be living there.'

I arrive within minutes of this exchange to find mum, red faced and seething as she sits on a chair in the kitchen, holding her chest. She is so angry that she cannot talk for a few minutes. While she is trying to catch her breath, I take advantage of the heavy silence.

'Mum, you would give her great pleasure if you die of a heart attack. I don't want you to give her that pleasure. Please, I am begging you to just ignore her as best you can. She is an evil bitch and takes great pleasure in watching your face go red.' I hug her. 'Are you okay now?' I turn as the kettle starts bubbling and make her a cup of tea. 'Mum, I don't know how we are all going to get through this. There does not seem to be a light at the end of the tunnel. I keep hoping they will bugger off and die, but they just seem to stick around like a bad smell.' I try and make light of the situation that we all find ourselves in.

'Jen, I hate her. She taunts the dogs until their yapping gets me out there. She comes three times a day, ordering Philly around, and poking her nose in my business. I feel sorry for Philly, because she is terrified of the harridan. She is worse than any abscess on the butt of humanity.' She has got her breath back.

'Oh Mum, you make me laugh.' I love her sense of humour. 'But seriously, short of tying you to the kitchen chair, I am begging you, to please not go out there. She is just waiting for the slightest excuse to retaliate against something you do or say. Age will not cut with her. She does not care and she would beat the living daylights out of you without a second thought. Just be very careful.' I stare out the window at the changing landscape, and narrowing my eyes at the shadows cowering under the trees.

Mud and thatch homes have risen up, hunched and frowning over our lands. The smell of wood fires fills the air every morning and evening, turning the sky from blue into a grey haze. Trees are fast disappearing, crudely axed down and torn apart, just like the freedom we have lived with over the past sixteen years. What the hell are we going to do? We can't just leave our farm to these people. We have invested our whole working lives into buying this farm, and many families depend on us.

'Oh, Mum, what are we going to do? They are becoming more and more demanding as the months go on. Please be careful of this woman. Bite your tongue, okay?' I take her hand, forcing her to look at me.

'I will try, Jen.'

'No Mum, you will. You heard what happened to John Melrose (an elderly fellow farmer). They tied him up and beat him with a whip. They then left him all trussed up. Mum, they don't care about us. They are out to get us.' I am stern.

The mornings are still sweet and warm as the sun lays a gentle caress across the garden. However Maggie and Adam go about their daily chores with long faces and bleeding hearts, knowing instinctively that we are all at a crossroad and it is just a matter of how long do we all have left on the farm? They are feeling the pressure of living under the constant threats from these people. The majority of the labour does not want the invasions, but there are a percentage of these people, who feel that if there is land going for free, they might as well peg out a plot for themselves. We are then being put in a position of whether they are then still employed. Jarent is a good example as we do not know how to play that one.

Our little group of geriatrics with grizzled beards and wobbly knees are vulnerable. We have a group of eight of these old men who are bent like capital C's and unable to do manual work, so we employ them as crop guards. They spend their days chasing baboon out of the various lands. Old men who sit, legs stretched out in the African dust enjoying the warmth of the sun as they bow in silent meditation.

Mikaela is home for her birthday. I look at the way her smile lights up the room and with the sunlight slanting through the window and outlining her body with a gilded aura; she is just perfect and beautiful. Ben, cocky and grinning widely hands her a small present, which she tears open revealing a lovely silver chain, which she immediately pops around her wrist. I watch these two and my mood lifts.

'This is crazy. You are 19 years old already Mikaela?' I am feeling bemused. 'A toast to you and here's wishing you many more happy years.' I raise my beer shandy and we all clink glasses. Ben had dragged her out early this morning, and they had gone for a long horse ride, keeping to the road and not straying too far from home.

'Thanks, Mum and Dad, and also thanks, Ben. I loved going for a ride this morning. It was magical being out early, and no one else seemed to be around hey, Ben.' She takes a long swig of her drink, bubbling with excitement. Maggie serves up a roast chicken with all the trimmings. It is mouth watering with its crisp brown skin and thick gravy but there is something missing from the meal. Maggie's face is dragged down with tension and her mood is as dark as a moonless night. She seems trapped in a miserable place of solitude and I am concerned about her. I listen to Mikaela and Ben's cheerful young voices and I drag my mind back to the present. I will have a chat with Maggie in the morning. We finish the meal, scraping every last little morsel off our plates and thanking Maggie, we move out onto the veranda which has been made warm and mellow by the afternoon sun. Gran and pa (my mum and dad) join us for tea and gooey chocolate cake. Dad's shoulders are stooped and he eases his bum onto the cushion clad metal garden chair. He has been a bit under the weather lately which is why they did not join us for lunch.

'You okay, Pa?' Mikaela asks, rubbing his leathery arm gently.

'I would be if I could get rid of this virus.'

'What virus are you talking about?' I join the conversation.

'The two legged virus that is attacking our very existence. I don't think there is an anti biotic that will cure this ailment and make me feel better.' He gives a wry little smile, but his grey eyes are weary and even his wiry hair has flopped over to one side, disgruntled and worn. After tea Gary nudges Mikaela and they both look at their watches. We don't want her leaving too late. She will drop Ben off at school on her way back to Harare.

Gary pops his arm around my shoulders, hugging me tight. It has been a great weekend with these two precious people and best of all, the radio has been quiet. Normality is a much needed commodity in our lives. The last week has been hell with constant calls over the radio. Desperate pleas for help from desperate farmers crushed under the heels of corrosion of the old order.

'Bye, guys... drive carefully.' We close the gate behind us and move back onto the veranda so we can watch them disappearing up the road. Mum and dad ease their aching backs before plodding slowly up the hill to their little cottage. The situation is taking its toll on them both. The niggling anxiety never leaves, day after day, it is there, lurking and waiting to pounce.

We sit out in the cool breeze enjoying the quietness as the day fades like a passing shadow. It is so peaceful. There is only the slight rustling of the trees as the breeze swings through the canopies, and the slight humming of midges as they hover around our feet. I turn to Gary smiling.

'It is so peaceful. What a perfect ending to Mikacla's birthday. That was such a lovely weekend. It was so good to hear them both laughing so much. This whole land grab been hard on them too, Gary. Ben worries himself silly at school. As you know, he is always phoning to find out if we are all okay, and on the day he doesn't phone, Mikaela does.' I stare out over the emerald lawn. 'I love my home, Gary. What are we going to do?' I wave my arm, 'all of this is so precious to me. I don't know how much longer we can go on living from day to day. These constant threats are so damn frightening.'

'I am concerned about the old man.'

'I know, Gary. Even his hair looks exhausted. I wish we could persuade them to go down to Richards (dad's brother) for a few days, but they are having endless bloody problems as well. I don't think there are many farmers in the country who don't have these people all over them like a frigging rash. The cracks are opening and I wish they would open wide enough to swallow every two legged squatter up. That would solve some issues.'

'Jen, I don't know what is going to happen to us all, but at this stage, I have to concentrate on planting this crop and paying off our overdraft.'

'It is not often that we have had such a peaceful day.' I smile touching my glass with his. The words are no sooner out my mouth and the distress call comes over the radio.

It is one of the district wives, Cheryl shrieking for someone to come and help. Fear pervades the room and I stand transfixed listening to the desperate screams of a fellow farmer's wife. I can feel her terror and my heart lurches painfully as it becomes clear that the war vets have her husband in the laundry section of the house. She has managed to lock herself in the bedroom: panic her only companion. Two of their farming neighbours leap into action, their voices calm as they plan to meet up and the top of the road. Reassuring Cheryl that they will be with her in about 8 minutes, they ask that the radio channel is left open.

The radio goes dead. We wait, staring at the radio. It is silent and sullen.

'Oh, Gary, I wonder what the hell is going on. They seem to be taking ages. Oh hell, I hope they are all okay.' I am pacing up and down the passage, my heart threatening to leap out of my chest.

The call eventually comes letting us know that they have Alan and Cheryl off the farm and are rushing them through to the hospital. The evening drags on. Gary and I wander through to the bathroom for a bath, for want of something to do. This sitting and waiting is a killer. The burble on the radio has us both airborne and down the passage. Standing stark naked with water dripping down onto the tiles, we listen to the update on Alan.

'Forty stitches to his head, a perforated ear drum, broken nose and fractured cheek bones. Alan also has a dislocated shoulder and a broken finger.' My bewildered gaze meets Gary's. He is shaking his head slowly and about to talk when the radio bursts forth again. 'Alan also has two shot gun pellets in the leg; he is covered in multiple bruises and cuts to the body and has an enormous boot print on his backside.'

I feel my stomach contracting as the rodents gnaw on my innards. This is a feeling that has become far too familiar.

The report on Alan's condition then finishes with the fact that he has also had a couple of finger nails pulled out.

'Oh my god! I feel sick.' I fly back to the bathroom and leaning over the toilet, I vomit, my frame heaving wretchedly as I lose the contents of my stomach.

'Jen, are you okay?' His voice is gentle as he takes me into his arms and cradles my head on his shoulders.

'What the hell are we all doing? What has happened that these people can just bully their way into our lives, committing such atrocious acts of violence, and no one seems to care, least of all these damn people.' I climb back into the bath, running the hot tap. 'Gary, this is never going to go away, is it? I am frightened, Gary. I don't see where we are going from here and I feel guilty because I sometimes just want to get the hell away from this farm. I am so confused because I love this place and I can't imagine not being here but at the same time, I am beginning to hate it.'

'No, I don't think that this is going to go away, Jen.' He stares at his face in the mirror, the scar a crushing reminder of how serious these people are. 'I see Prof. Levy in two weeks time.'

'Good Gary, you need to ask him to patch up that hole, and fast. Things are happening so quickly now. There are incidents every other day. People we know being murdered, others hurt.' I wash my face and then grabbing the sponge, I scrub my body trying to cleanse away the dust of this raw and violent place. 'Is this what the world of farming is all about now? Being tortured in our own homes? Where is the justice?' The tremor in my voice is drowned out by a low grumble of thunder. 'No one cares about Zimbabwe. No one cares about us, the opposition and the labour.'

The echo of harmony is lost in the storm of political currents.

A few days later we hear that Alan is also having to undergo treatment for Aids as one these bastards had bitten his finger until it

123

broke. His feet had also been so badly burnt that it was going to be a while before he would make a full recovery from his violent encounter with the local 'farm invaders' or war vets.

Chapter 19

MOVING OUR GOAL POSTS

Maggie is flagging. We are edging towards the last month of the year 2000. I can't pin point what is troubling her, which sounds stupid as we are all living under extreme stress. There is a dull grey hue to her face. The bounce has long gone out of her step. I give her a bottle of multi vitamins with instructions on how many to take a day. I am hoping that these supplements will help to boost her up. Every morning, she makes up a tasty soup for the domestic workers to have with their bread at tea, and she is an avid buyer of Mum's broiler chickens so I know she is eating well. The clinic in the district has been unable to diagnose any problem and so we decide that like the rest of us, she is living on her nerves.

Gary's operation has all gone to plan. Prof. Levy has taken bone from his hip, building up the dent in his forehead, affording some added protection. We can no longer see the 'hole on his forehead breathing.'

Our crops are in the ground; planted under extreme harassment from the war vets. We and the labour are like exhausted moths bashing our wings against invisible prison bars that cage our minds. Our farming district is dogged by long shadows and weary strides. Incidents of violence are becoming a part of our daily lives as the weeks fly past leaving behind the distinctly pungent stench of ZANU PF thugs.

'Oh Gary, there have been some awful reports about farmers' dogs being hung on the security gates by hooks and left to die. Kids ponies having hooves chopped off to show what can happen to the farmers.' I am hissing with ire. 'I don't have any names but where there is smoke there is fire.' He grabs my shoulders, shaking me gently.

'Jen, come now, let us go and sit down. You have to understand that rumours could be rife, but we cannot underestimate these bastards. Like I have said before, we cannot sneeze at these people, they are cruel and they mean business. They want our land and our homes. We have to keep our heads.' He hugs me. 'Okay?' I nod, gulping for air; the hissing has given way to angry tears.

'What about our animals?' I blow my nose. 'All our horses and the cattle are vulnerable too. I will be murderous if they kill Stripes. She has defied death by jumping off the lorry so many times now. She is part of this farm and will grow old here. While cows have come and gone, mostly to cold storage, she continues to leave her footprints, a legend in her on rights.'

'Jen, Stripes is such an aggressive cow, I like to think that nobody could get close enough to do her any harm.' He smiles with pride. 'This cow has outwitted us on many occasions.'

'I know she has, Gary. I just cannot bear to think of the cruelty that has been shown to the wild life and the farm animals.'

The middle of December is suddenly upon us. The air is hot and steamy and the trees and wind whisper their thoughts as we watch the clear blue skies, praying for the sight of clouds. The lack of rain used to be our biggest fear.

I worry about my mum and dad, who are in their seventies; frail and vulnerable people whose futures are now in the hands of these hate filled war vets. Mugabe's latest inflammatory speech while addressing delegates at the annual ZANU PF congress accuses the whites of destroying the economy. He said ' Our party must continue to strike fear into the heart of the white man. They must tremble…'

We hear over the radio communications of a farmer in Bulawayo (in the west of the country) receiving a written death threat which reads 'Your friend Martin was our breakfast for Christmas'. Martin Olds had been murdered in the previous April. A hot flickering of anger and frustration burns like a coal fire deep in the pit of my stomach and I stamp out onto the sun drenched veranda, staring out over my garden, trying to control my emotions. Gary, Mikaela and Ben follow me out and the four of us stand with our hands clenched around the burglar bars. 'There are not enough stones to kick in this garden.' I turn to Gary. 'How many of our war veterans are armed?' The words are no sooner out my mouth and I laugh cynically because they have now become 'our' war veterans.

On December 31st 2000, we join friends down at the country club on New Year's Eve where we become stubborn survivors of the long night, opening our throats and drowning our worries.

'Eight months of living with our unwanted visitors.' Holding up a glass and downing the remains of his drink, Gary orders another round. A group of us move out onto the lawn, huddling close together to watch the orange glow of dawn struggle through the thick blanket of tempestuous clouds bubbling on the horizon. We are not entirely convinced that this is the bright promise of a new year for Zimbabweans, so we drink to good tobacco prices and surviving another season.

The bone graft done on Gary's forehead has been re-absorbed by his body. Prof. Levy had warned us that this could happen. He now faces another visit to the operating theatre, but he cringes at the thought.

The state has withdrawn all charges against the war veteran suspected of murdering Dave Stevens, apparently due to a lack of evidence.

'What lack of evidence hey Gary? You shoot someone in front of a crowd of people and then poof, it all just disappears. Sure... I have never heard such hot bubbling rocking horse shit in my life. I would say any evidence is hidden deep in a file in some fat bastard's filing cabinet. He has probably thrown away the key.' I am seething. I kick the burglar bar on the veranda (my favourite kicking post), wincing as pain shoots through my big toe. 'Ouch, that was bloody sore. Right, I have had my say, let's go and kill a few golf balls. Sometimes I wish we could just go away.'

'Jen, our whole lives are tied up in this farm. We can't just leave all our responsibilities behind us.'

'I know, Gary. We have the folks, the kids, the horses, dogs and 101 families depending on making a living on the farm. I know all that. I am just dreaming.' I kick the bar again.

Chapter 20

THE VULTURES

Gary's footsteps pound down the passage, his voice urgent. 'Quick, Jen lets go. Call the kids. There are vultures circling on the top section.'

'Vultures..?' I pop out from the bathroom. 'Which vultures are you talking about, Gary? The feathered ones with wings or do you mean the two legged ones with frizzy hair? Are they coming in for the kill?' He raises one eyebrow.

'Jen, seriously, the vultures are forming a stack in the sky. Move your butt, let's go, or will miss the feast.'

The four of us jump in the green twin cab. The trees flash past as we roar up the narrow road to the top section. The top section plateaus out and there are roughly 3 500 hundred acres for as far as the eye can see; beautiful flat lands that appear to drift into the pale blue Inyanga Mountains in the far distance. A wonderful mountainous scene; mellowed into a warm glow by the shadows of the afternoon sun. We drive through the tobacco land, slowing down to a crawl as we follow behind the tractor and trailer piled high with freshly reaped tobacco. The sickly sweet odour of tobacco leaves hangs in the air, and turning to Gary I burst out laughing. We are so in tune with our thoughts.

'That is the smell of money.' He removes his hands from the steering wheel, rubbing them together like Fagan. 'Look at it, Jen, piles of money bouncing around in front of your eyes. Well there it is and let's hope for a good selling season.' The green and yellow duvet cover of tobacco bounces gently as the tractor negotiates the rough dirt road, and the loaded trailer sways behind. It turns off up one of the contours and parks. Gary waves in return to a greeting from the driver. At the end of the tobacco land we turn off the road onto a track that leads down through the trees towards what we call 'spook dam'. Spook dam is a spring that never dries up and causes great consternation amongst the labour. They tell stories of a ghostly presence in the vicinity, of smoky breezes rattling the branches of the trees and unearthly shadows rising through the mist. 'Spook Dam' and the immediate area around it are left untouched and alone to the mercy of its night time visitors. Mikaela, Ben and I have our windows down and we are all sitting on the sills with our bums hanging out and our feet on the seats, scanning the skies. We pass close by the burbling spring that appeases the restless spirits.

'There they are Dad, over there'. Ben's excitement is contagious and he is pointing, a huge grin on his face, white teeth flashing against his brown skin. 'Six minutes, Dad. Not bad driving.' He teases. There they are swirling in circles, aeroplanes in a stack waiting to land. 'Wow, look, there are loads of them. That is the most amazing sight.'

We find the carcass. It is a sable. I am devastated as it has been snared and a ghastly wound weeps sickly yellow pus. I feel anger bubbling in the deep pit of my stomach. We had a herd of sixty odd sables that wander through the various farms in the district, roaming through the open woodland grazing peacefully. But for them, life too has changed. The farm occupations have led to lawlessness and poaching has become a popular sport. The herd of sable are declining. Gary jumps out the truck, and pulling his Swiss army knife out of his pocket, he slits open the carcass for the vultures, gagging as the decaying smell of death assaults his nostrils. I turn away as the spurt of berry-red blood spills out onto the dried earth turning the surrounding patches of grass into a crimson battle ground. 'Oh my, God... the stench.' He lurches backwards. 'It just gets to me. It is putrid' he is holding his hand over his nose, heaving uncontrollably as the bile rises up his throat, and he bends over with hands planted firmly on his knees. Climbing back into the vehicle, the smell clings to his clothes prompting us all to stick our heads out the windows. He reverses the truck back, parking under a low hanging msasa tree; far enough away to not be intruding but close enough to have a front row seat for one of natures' finest shows.

We sit transfixed, as the vultures circle before falling out of the sky, one after the other and landing with perfect, but noisy precision. With their dark legs on terra firma they wobble, looking ungainly as they half close their wings, flapping rapidly and aggressively. The dark brown eyes of the vultures assess the situation, greedy for the taste of carrion. They approach the carcass, their bald heads pushed forward and their long necks forming the perfect S bend. With heads stained crimson, they bicker and screech at each other. The smell of blood is over powering and my stomach churns, revolting against the stench; in turn the large vultures become uncontrollably excited. Shouting vile curses at each other, they launch forward attacking the carcass.

'White Back Vultures I am certain. We will check when we get home' Gary answers the question that foremost on our minds. I am glued.

'Oh my word, look at that one there.' I point at a large medieval soldier. 'Look, he looks just like a grizzled old soldier with a beaked nose. I would not like to get in the way of that beak, it is lethal.'

'We could call him pa.' Mikaela gives us an evil grin. 'Well pa also has a beaked nose.' She bursts out laughing. 'Sometimes, he even hunches his shoulders.'

'He does not bicker though.' Ben adds his little bit. We all have a laugh at my dear old dad's expense, and Mikaela leans over running her finger down my beaked nose, nudging Ben in the ribs and pointing at me.

'Mama Vulture, a tough old bird.' She tickles me. We all turn our attention back to the feeding frenzy. This is nature, at her most spectacular. The raucous squabbling climaxes when a couple of black backed jackals, yipping and quivering with excitement try nosing in for a morsel. With much screeching and wing flapping they are chased away.

'Gary, look how those sneaky little critters just keep out of range of those razor sharp beaks. Look at how they wait patiently on the perimeter, making do with a few scraps that are dropped by the birds.' I am totally absorbed. 'Shame, I feel a little sorry for them.'

'They are sneaky little animals and one of the biggest rabies carriers as they feed on all carrion.' Gary whispers.

'Dad, this has been amazing. I wonder how far they have come.' Mikaela keeps her tone low.

'I am not sure. Hundreds of kilometres, but we will look it up when we get home.' Gary answers her, not taking his eyes off the melee.

'I am hoping that the resident hyenas might show up, Gary. How exciting would that be? You know, we are so damn lucky to have this abundance of wild life right on our back door.' I leave it at that as I don't want to think of the future right now.

A comfortable silence hangs in the car, enveloping us all in a heavy, intoxicating atmosphere. Nature at her finest and I drift in the stream of the bush, content and for the moment full of unblemished optimism.

We all keep our eyes peeled; they might just come like thieves in the night, led by their lust for meat. This is easy pickings for the hyena that move on and off our farm. They are a real menace to ours and our neighbour's cattle, their giggles eerie and haunting in the dark of night, as the cattle herd together, protecting their young. Large heads, round ears and sloping backs don't bypass Jim's (the crop guard) keen eye, and he often spots them melting away into the long grass. Their sense of smell, hearing and sight are acute and the four of us sit quietly, hoping to hear the 'whoop whoop' call which starts low and ends high, a chilling sound to say the least. If they don't come soon, they will most certainly be dropping by later; but the carcass will be clean bones by then. The hyenas do not arrive and we decide to leave the noisy banquet. This show has been balm on our weary and over burdened spirits. It's been magical.

We retrace our tracks through the bush leaving the noisy party behind. Bumping slowly over the rough road through the tobacco lands we meet up with a group of war vets. The carefree ambience in the car evaporates into thin air; my heart starts to beat uncontrollably.

Their dark sweaty faces glare at us as we negotiate our way through the human wall. Slapping the back of the vehicle with their open palms is not doing any damage to the vehicle; but my heart rate edges up a notch, shooting acid up my throat. My fingers grope for the packet of antacid tablets and I chew greedily trying to calm my damaged spirit.

The trip home is done in brooding silence.

Chapter 21

MAGGIE'S MOMENT

We have crept through the winter months with jerseys wrapped firmly around our bodies, keeping out the cold wind as it whistles a mournful tune. We have again, planted seedbeds for the next crop of tobacco, causing anger with our resident war vets. We are caught up in a political current that ripples and rolls into darkness as they create havoc by blocking tractors and labour from going to work. The winter months have been scarred by the continual harassment of citizens country wide and Gary's shoulders droop with a dejected air as he stands, with hands on his hips staring at row upon row of withered seedbeds.

I look up as Gary appears, slouching back against the dining room wall, arms folded defensively across his chest. He stares at me through eyes that are bruised and swollen again. We arrived home yesterday. He has had a second operation to try and build up his forehead.

'What is the matter, Gary? Has something happened?' One look at his body language leaves me in no doubt that something is troubling him.

'Prof. Levy has made me look like a fucking rhino, and now the poachers are probably going to get me.' He looks so woebegone that I burst out laughing.

'What on earth are you talking about?'

'He has made me look like a fucking rhino, Jen.' His hand is feeling the discoloured bandage covering his head. 'I had a look this morning and ....' He slowly unwinds the bandage and points 'look'. I can feel my eyes widening in shock. His forehead protrudes out in an alarming way. He looks positively Neanderthal. 'You see, look at your face. My forehead looks horrendous.'

'Gary, yes, it does. But let's just think logically about this.'

'Logical thought. At this present point in time there is no logic.'

'Gary, listen.' I shake his shoulders. 'The bone from your hip was reabsorbed the last time, and this time around he is taking no chances, so he has given you extra...' I am desperately trying to keep my face devoid of expression. It looks awful, and I start to laugh. 'He has...,' I wheeze,' 'given you a horn.'

'Oh shut up, Jen.' And then he cannot hold the rumble that forces its way up his throat, bursting out with gusto. I wrap my arms around him, squeezing him tight.

'I won't let the poachers anywhere near you.' I bend over resting my hands on my knees, breathless as we both laugh hysterically. Within a week, the bone is already being reabsorbed and Gary begins to look more like a modern day man.

We are coming to the end of our journey on this farm. Tractors are parked in the workshop area. The labourers stay close to their huts. A silence spreads its wings over the land and I continue to write letters; pages of inadequate words of condolences to farmers' wives whose husbands have been beaten or murdered. One of our neighbours has had a gun held to his head insisting that they have to stop all farming operations; our fields stand empty as a whisper of restlessness brushes our faces with a feverish kiss.

Maggie's dark face is drawn. I am sitting on the veranda steps, watching the road. I pat the step next to me and she plonks down, her breath expelling loudly like an old pair of bagpipes. We sit with our legs stretched out, enjoying the feel of the warm sun. War veterans, like an army of ants march over the lands and Maggie turns to me.

'What are we going to do?' She snorts, shaking her head. 'I am scared, Miss Jeans.'

'Maggie, I don't know. The boss, he is very worried because these people are not going to let us plant the tobacco. The vegetables for export, they are rotting now.' I stare up the road and into the fields towards the people who are causing such misery. 'Maggie, what did the clinic say to you?'

'They have given me more aspirin, for my legs are sore and very heavy.'

'Would you like to see my doctor?'

'No, Miss Jeans. The aspirin helps the ache. Maybe it is nearly my time.'

'Maggie, don't talk like that.' I shiver and she smiles. She leans over rubbing her dark calves that are dry and textured like knobbly old branches.

'I am just tired, Miss Jeans.' I stare at the hair that is escaping from her dook (head scarf); it is as brittle as dry winter grass.

'I want you to go off this afternoon. Go and rest. Edna can cope here in the house, Maggie.' We smile at each other as we both know that Edna has a job in the house, more for her than me. 'Go and find your laughter again and when you do, then you can come back to work. It will be sick leave okay?' Her eyes brim, and I pat her shoulder. 'Go on, I need you to get better as we both need to get old together and sit like this all day long.' She pushes herself up, grunting with effort, and I can hear her feet slapping the floor as she trudges through to the lounge. I close my eyes, holding my breath, leaping with fright when I feel a hand on my shoulder. Her words have put the wind up me.

'Miss Jeans, thank you.' She is staring down at me and I find I am seeing behind her mask, and there is pain and fear. I jump to my feet and we both stand quietly, and for a moment I see a reflective glow in her eyes, like a light from heaven. My heart misses a beat and then the glow has gone.

'No Maggie, it is me who needs to thank you.' An emotional lump, the size of a large juicy apple has lodged itself in my throat and hot tears threaten to spill. 'You have done so much for me. Thank you.' She smiles and I watch her leave, patting the dogs fondly as she passes them.

The bush is alive, a gorgeous canvas of reds, russets, creamy wheat and browns. The south east wind whistles and blows, snaking through the long grass and adding to the vulnerability of the landscape; this is every farmer's nightmare time of the year. Fire season is with us again. For a few months of the year the msasa trees grace us with their magnificent show of colours; absolutely startling and sheer glory to look at. I am passionate about the African bush. Driving back down the hill after a morning's shopping in Marondera; anger erupts as I can see evidence of our beautiful trees being recklessly felled. Bare, brown patches of earth are appearing like a blot on the landscape. We know that this felling has been going on for the past year. I seem to have closed my eyes to it all, but today, I see everything. As farmers, we don't have a leg to stand on. We are unable to put a stop to this destruction.

The labour force, huddle together in small groups, their thin shoulders touching. They talk in quiet urgent tones on how they are going to feed their families, if and when we leave the farm. We are all being chased by the dark that is descending over the farm. The war vets are like mambas. There is no antidote, given that the police won't arrest them, as they say that all cases pertaining to farms are political. Worry is gnawing away at my stomach. Gary and the labour are under tremendous stress and of course there is Maggie. I just want her back at work and laughing.

It is two weeks since our conversation on the steps. Every day I have made up a soup and send it over to Maggie. Gift, the driver has taken her back to the clinic this morning. On her return, I take her some soup. Rapping quietly on her door, I enter the room.

'Hello, Maggie. How are you feeling today?' She is resting on her mattress on the floor. 'Can I come in?'

'Hello, Miss Jeans.' She beckons me. I sit cross legged on the floor next to the mattress looking around at her meagre belongings. 'The clinic, they have given me some more aspirin.'

'Oh.' I expel my breath. I feel angry with the clinic. The room is spotless and small piles of folded clothes sit on top of a small chest of drawers. A faint whiff of wood smoke hangs like silky cobwebs from the rafters. On a wooden dining chair next to the mattress is an old china ewer full of water and an empty blue glass. She drags herself up using the wall as a back rest; she makes an effort to drink the nourishing soup. I am frowning and endeavour to clear my face of expression; a difficult thing to do as I watch her trembling hand holding the cup of soup attempting it's epic journey from her knee to her dry mouth. She waves my hand away, refusing help and after a few sips; I take the cup from her fingers, placing it on the floor.

'Maggie, Mikaela and Ben keep asking how you are. They are hoping you will soon be back in the kitchen talking to the fish, and yes Beans and Toffee are missing you too.' I am aware that I am prattling away. She smiles, eyes half closed and I keep my voice low.

138

'I am sure Hussan has told you that the tractors are still not working and that the Government has given us a Section 8' (the order from Government to leave the farm within 30 days.) I pick an imaginary thread off my denim clad knee, 'but we will be okay, and you and Hussan will come with us. We will also take Adam and Edna.' She nods her head tiredly and I stop talking, enjoying a comfortable silence. A gentle snore quivers in the air and I quietly get to my feet, touching her briefly on the shoulder. She is our maid and she is my friend. I feel desperately sad that she has been living under such stress and I am extremely worried about her.

The following morning I am picking some flowers in the garden. A dark foreboding shadow falls across the flowerbed and I turn around feeling the goose bumps prickling my neck. Edna's shoulders are drooped, tears cascade down her cheeks and she sobs silently, her chest heaving. My heart starts pumping wildly, my mind shouting no to the answer of the question that I know is in my eyes.

'Oh no, Edna, I am so sorry about your mum.' My voice is choked with tears. I can feel my chest heaving, as wave after wave of emotion rolls up into my throat. 'No....'

'Hussan came and called me at 3 o'clock this morning and she died at 5.30ish.' She blows her nose. 'We were with her, Madam.' She is looking at me, her eyes blank. The thin line between life and death is foremost on my mind. I feel certain of a light caress across my cheek and look around startled. Maggie is saying farewell before floating away on her spiritual journey to higher plains where she will find peace. We wander back through the sweet smelling jasmine arch and I flop down onto the front step, patting the space next to me. Edna sits. The two bitches squeeze in between us and we both wrap an arm around a dog, united in our grief.

'Edna, the boss will pay for all funeral expenses so you do not need to worry about that.' I trumpet loudly into my tissue, 'you must go home now and do what you need to do. I know that she will want to be buried on her plot in the homelands. Gift will pick up a coffin and then he will take your mum and Hussan and you to her homelands. You let me know of the arrangements.' I pat her knee. 'Your mother was a good woman.' I reflect that Maggie can only be about 43 years of age. 'Give her a good send off.' I hand her the glorious bunch of freshly picked flowers. 'Take a vase and put these in your house.' It is a tradition of ours to give flowers.' I listen to her heavy footsteps dragging her grief with her through the house, and putting my head onto my knees, I sob noisily.

'Oh Gary, we always wanted to grow old and sit in the sun, and now she has gone. There is a huge hole in my chest.' I lean my head against his shoulder, grateful that he has dashed back to the house, arriving within minutes of Hussan telling him. Mum and dad pop down from their cottage, and Adam calls both Hussan and Edna so the folks can also offer them their condolences.

Our house feels like an empty shell after Maggie died. Where there was noise and laughter, there is now solitude. She had filled my days with quips and laughter for close on fifteen years now. I feel sad that I am never going to hear 'Miss Jeans' ever again.

This is a start of the new chapter in all our lives. I miss her, we all miss her. Maggie had great faith and I know that she has finished her journey of life. I now understand that for the last couple of months she has also been 'Homeward Bound.'

Chapter 22

OUR EQUINE FRIENDS

Over the years we have invested in some beautiful polo crosse horses for Mikaela and Ben to pursue their total love of this sport. We have Mary, a beautiful mare, copper, sleek and shiny. She gallops as fast as the wind, her hooves barely touching the ground as she races down the field. Mary had belonged to Squack Whaley (one of the local farmers), an extremely talented player and rider, whose knowledge of schooling horses certainly showed in our lucky find. Amusalto, a gelding wearing a glossy dark coat had also belonged to Squack. He is a large and powerful horse, beauty without vanity as he struts through the paddock adding richness and finesse to the herd. Ben is firm and strong with him and I believe in another year, these two will have the perfect partnership on the field. Elusive, a gorgeous mare, with a large liquid eye and sleek rippling muscles is gentle as she moves like a dancer to music only she can hear. She is being schooled by Mikaela and Ben and will be ready for the following polo crosse season.

A team comprises of six players to a side and divided into two sections of three; number 1 who is the attack, number 2 who covers the centre and number 3 who is the defence. Each chukka takes between six to eight minutes. The two opposing teams line up in the centre of the field and the umpire throws the ball into play. The player who catches the ball with his racket (a light weight cane stick with a net, that pockets back and front) rides off or passes to team members as they gallop towards the goal posts. The ball cannot be carried over the penalty line in front of the goal posts. The number one needs to bounce it over the line and throw it through the goals to score. The game comprises of six chukkas and each side of a team will play three chukkas. At the end of the final chukka, the total aggregate of goals scored throughout the game by the two sections constitutes the final score.

I join the mish mash of spectators sitting on the side line. We all lean forward, necks craning and voices uniting. We are a colourful collection of hats, sunglasses and brightly patterned tops, children laughing and sweet wrappers. The delicious odour of hamburgers, steak rolls and hotdogs hovers in the air, enticing our taste buds. Crowds of hungry people bite into fresh rolls oozing with tomato sauce and various other condiments. This all makes for a rowdy backdrop against which the players and their horses play the game under the clear blue winter sky.

I sit amongst friends, my hat pulled low over my forehead and shielding my eyes from the sun. My voice is hoarse from shouting and the palms of my hands feel sweaty as I watch the horses gallop up and down the field. The thundering of hooves and the clashing of polo crosse sticks reverberates around the field, and the referee's whistle, high pitched and persistent stops play momentarily before the action starts again. After a chukka, the horses are led around behind the goal posts, neighing gently as their girths are loosened and the grooms wipe them down, whispering quietly to them, and keeping them calm. Dust swirls around the field clogging your nostrils and settling in a fine sprinkling over your clothes. The sweet smell of leather, horse sweat and smoke from the various braais (barbeques) around the camp hangs in the air. An excited cheer from the home crowd lights a spark of enthusiasm in the players to win their chukka, as they fight for the ball, scooping it up into the net and passing it with perfect precision for the number one to catch and score. It is an exciting spectators sport and I never cease to be amazed watching the power of these wonderful creatures. With veins bulging, nostrils flaring and muscles rippling they spray up clouds of dust as horse and rider become one, moulding together to win the game. It is a marvellous partnership of strength and beauty. I watch and admire, and in a small way envy the way these riders unite with their horses and their heartbeats become one. It is poetry in motion.

Mikaela has this amazing ability to connect with the horses and she spends many happy hours working in the ring, honing up on her Monty Roberts skills. She loves to take Prince out on outrides on the farm, normally with one arm around her little jack Russell bitch sitting on the saddle in front of her. Beetle's pink tongue lolls out in happiness and Mikaela's facial expression matches the little dogs, only minus the lolling tongue. Prince, a grey Arab sports a thick plumy tail as he treads carefully, ears twitching as he listens to Mikaela's gentle murmurs and I watch, shaking my head as they disappear through the trees. Beetle sits calmly in front of her, long body pressed into Mikaela, and the three of them make a strange picture, one that definitely needs putting away in the memory bank. A drowsy murmur floats in the air as I leave the paddock and make my way through the workshop area to the house. Prince has been part of the family for ten years now and when in his company, Mikaela is in heaven. The dust swirls around the school as the horses, muscles rippling, canter around the ring and the strong smell of horse manure and sweat clings to my clothes. I wipe a dusty forearm over my forehead feeling earthy and content.

These are all the gentle creatures, plus a few hangers on, one that we have saved from making the dreaded voyage to the croc farm. They idle their days away, grazing on the lush grass. They are all different in temperament and speed, treading softly on the bottom section of the farm, leaving hoof prints in the sand and a song in our hearts.

I am tossing and turning, dragging the duvet cover with me and driving Gary nuts as we have a perpetual 'war of the duvet' at night. My mind is restless, disturbed with worry over our equine friends. I know what we are going to have to do. With farmers having to leave their land, horses are adding another tragic dimension to the land grab. There are thousands of horses that need re homing and no one to take them on.

'Gary, who is going to want to take on our horses, I am having nightmares about them. There are so many farmers having to leave their farms, and there will be hundreds of horses needing re-homing.' I am having difficulty in controlling the wobble in my voice.

'Jen, we are not going to do anything about them yet. We have put the word out there and someone will want them.' His calm demeanour gives me hope.

'Okay, Gary. I don't really know what I am asking you to do. I do not want to have them all destroyed, but will do it if we have to. The stories of cruelty make my skin crawl. We are not going to leave any living pet behind if and when we go.' I feel enormous pressure building in my chest. 'We also have an aviary of birds that will need re-homing, or we will have to do something about them too.'

'Jen, we will tie up all the loose ends before we go. These people are not letting us farm, and we can't continue like this. I am paying the labour to sit around. I don't know how long we can keep this up. I suppose I know deep down... this is it, the end.'

'No..., oh I don't know. It's the not knowing that gets to me, Gary. I am relieved that all the cattle, save Stripes have gone to the abattoirs. At least, there are no worries there.' I know he is heart sore at the destruction of his small herd of breeding cows that we have built up over the years. 'You know, Gary, they are going to take everything from us. What about our equipment? What are we going to do?'

'Jen, I am not sure. I don't want to piss these guys off. They seem to have total control of our lives. If we go, we need to be able to take our equipment with us. I don't know who will want to buy it though, but I am buggered if I will leave it for these people.'

The phone call eventually comes. Our friend Anna from Rusape is going to take three of our horses, hopefully for re-homing. The two polo crosse horses will go back to their original owner. The two remaining horses, Basil and Mercy are going to have to be shot, but we just cannot face making this decision just yet.

We leave the farm early one morning. The mist swirls around the valley shrouding the trees, transparent and elusive as we drive slowly, headlights on to the top of the road. Far above the mist, the sun will soon be riding, high and golden in the sky, spreading warmth over our valley that has long since lost its tranquillity. We have a meeting/interview in Harare with a man from Mauritius.

A potential job offer is in the making. Hiding a smile I shake his hand, not daring to make eye contact with Gary. For those of you who used to watch the A Team, we could have been talking to B.A. Baracus with the exception being that this man is a Mauritian Indian not a Negro. His neck is adorned with countless heavy gold chains which nestle snugly against his chest, entangling one another amongst the course dark hairs that escape from the confines of the collared shirt. He jingles noisily as he moves. Large gold rings sit squat and foursquare on pudgy fingers and being of a gregarious nature he flaps his hands this way and that way explaining what this interview is all about. I drag my eyes over full pink lips, a large aquiline nose up to meet his dark brown eyes. His eyes are deep set, heavy lidded beneath shaggy eyebrows. A mop of thick dark hair, sits untamed and unruly on his large head. He is offering us a job in a soft voice. His manner is persuasive. Him and his business partner, Nan has land in Mauritius, and the means to lease more, should we require it. We need to do some research as they wish to venture into ostrich farming, that they will finance and we will manage.

'Money is no object. We would like your expertise on farming ostriches and we will provide the necessary means for you to run a successful project.' He smoothes out the creases in his napkin with his feminine hands that look startlingly dark against his crisp white shirt.

'We will go home and give this some serious thought. Once we have some ideas, we will be in contact. If we go ahead with this, you will not be disappointed. That I can promise you' Gary tells him. I can almost hear the cogs turning in his brain, and I look forward to us being alone so that we can talk.

We agree that once we have a proposition, Gary and I will take a trip out to Mauritius, have a look at the land, meet the other partner and then discuss things from there. Two and a half hours and countless cups of coffee later, we adjourn the meeting on a sweaty handshake. Once he has jingled his way past the other diners, his long shiny winkle picker shoes treading softly on the wooden floor as he minces towards the exit, Gary and I pull a face at each other grinning.

'Will his partner be Hannibal with his cigar, Face with his smooth talk or the lunatic Mad Murdock? Did you notice his ring, Gary? Well that was one smooth dude.' I joke.

'Jen, we can come up with something really good to put on the table.' His brain is working overtime. 'We will speak to him next week. It will be exciting to get our teeth into something, which will keep us busy. We will chat often to him and at least that will keep dialogue open. We have absolutely nothing to lose and you never know, you might find me extremely alluring when I join the A team', Gary's grin is infectious.

'It is good to see you excited again, Gary.'

146

'The breeze from the window certainly kept that strong smell of garlic circulating but I am sure a sea breeze will soften the blow. What do you think' he smiles. I wrinkle my nose in distaste.

'That smell of garlic was certainly not alluring. Do you want some more coffee or should we go home?' Gary cocks his head

'Let's bugger off home.'

We have six weeks to look into it and come up with relevant plans, before taking a trip to Mauritius. Feeling excited on our drive home, we discuss different ideas for our future by the sea. As we turn off onto the farm road, we look at each other. The reality of our situation is back. Oh God, are we really going to have to leave our farm? I am dreading tomorrow. Tomorrow is the day that the horses will be leaving. As we crest the hill, our valley is bathed in afternoon sunshine; I feel that I am staring down on a vanishing world.

The following morning I am up bright and early as Anna will be with us at about ten o'clock. She is coming to load up some of our precious horses. Adam has the horses in the schooling ring and they have all been groomed and fed. Adam and I are standing talking and I see him glance up the road, pointing. The lorry is slowly cresting the hill and moving cautiously down the long dirt road; followed closely by a cloud of dust swirling and rising behind it. I pop my arms around Prince's neck and snuggle my face into his mane, caressing him under his chin and marvelling at the softness of his skin. Taking a deep breath, I inhale deep into my chest trying to keep the smell of him with me: molasses, musk, leather and sunshine is how I will always remember Prince. I blink madly, trying to stop the tears welling but to no avail. I wipe my face, popping my sunglasses back on. I turn to the other horses sharing out my love. Smelling each in turn and then straightening my back, I ask Adam 'Please mhanya workshop and daidza boss' (please run to the workshop and call the boss).

Before he has time to turn on his heel, Gary comes striding around the corner, cap on head, but minus the large grin. Like me, he is feeling trapped. Things are moving too fast now, no longer in our control. Anna steps out of the lorry, pushing her cap off her forehead, she greets us both.

'Let's get these horses loaded.' She bustles around, throwing instructions Adam's way. 'Jen, I will look after them. They are all lovely horses, and I am sure we will be able to find good homes for them.' I again feel hot tears welling up, burning my eyes.

'We cannot thank you enough Anna.' I mumble. 'Without your help, I just don't know what we would do. Things are happening quickly now. We need to get our lives sorted out. We can't go on like we are.' There is nothing else to say.

I stand and watch as Anna drives slowly up the hill with our precious horses. My muddled mind is weighed down with so many different emotions. I become aware that my hands are clenched so tight that my knuckles are aching. I try to breathe slowly and deeply before rolling my shoulders and relaxing. Holding my hands up to my nose, I can still smell the distinctive musky scent of these wonderful animals, lingering with me. I watch the lorry until it disappears from sight. I look over my shoulder at Adam. He is standing with his shoulders slumped and his head hanging. His eyes are downcast, watching his gumboots as they scuff a line back and forth in the sand. He is totally unaware of me. His body is taut with pent up emotion. We stand silently side by side; despair clutching the air around us, boxing us in. The two remaining horses neigh loudly; confused at being abandoned in the field. The mournful sound is distressing and I can feel my heart hammering noisily against my rib cage as I watch Basil and Mercy smelling the air and pawing the ground. Stripes, our cheeky cow chews the cud, totally unaware of her destiny.

Mikaela and Ben are devastated with the news that their horses have actually gone now. Life will have to go on. We cannot thank Anna Bekker enough for all that she has done for us.

I would like to take time to remember Anna, who sadly after a tragic riding accident, was in a coma for a long time before passing on. She will always be remembered with great affection.

The date that Anna came to the farm to pick up the horses was the 12/09/2001. The tragedy of 9/11 is something that the world is desperately trying to get their minds around. Our personal loss seems so small in comparison to what had taken place at the Twin Towers. We had returned from our meeting in Harare and, like the rest of the world, we had sat in stunned disbelief as we watched the 'twin towers' crumble and we could not begin to imagine the chaos and fear surrounding this tragedy.

Chapter 23

DREAM CATCHERS

Many hours have been spent bending our brains on what we think will be the perfect project for the land that Nan owns in Mauritius. My brother Ken has flown up from Johannesburg to visit us. While he is with us, we view some houses in Marondera and put the old folks' names down for a house in Borrowdaille Trust, the Old Age Home in Marondera. Ken's banking brain leaps into action and with his help, we 'brain storm' over the finishing touch of the project for Mauritius.

'We plan to breed them, sell the meat, tan the hides and find a market for the feathers.' Gary recites his proposal, pointing at the relevant figures and pictures that we have compiled.

'Sounds excellent, Gary.' I shoot some questions his way, laughing at his smooth reply. 'Well that should soothe the way, Gary. I think we are done.'

Weeks of work have gone into our proposed project, and we cannot wait to fly into this exotic island destination. We are both feeling energized and excited again. All too soon Ken is leaving and we pack our bags, shoving in beach wear, shorts and sandals. We spend the night with Mikaela and the following morning board our flight for Mauritius.

Beautiful golden beaches and aquamarine water is my first view of this exquisite island. I lean over Gary, peering out the small window at the visual feast below. I grin with pleasure at Gary.

'Imagine living with that scenery.' I try to forget that we are circling the airport. I am clutching his hand tightly, cutting off the blood supply to his fingers and turning them white. I am not the best flyer. The runway at Mauritius is short and we come in fast, brakes squealing loudly and the plane crabs sideways. I close my eyes, screwing up my face and Gary laughs at me, rubbing the top of my head as unwittingly, I have assumed the crash position.

'No need for that, Jen, we have stopped,' he pulls my leg and I giggle self consciously, straightening my body, relieved that the plane has skidded to a halt.

'I was just checking my toes and if needs be, I was going to kiss my backside goodbye,' I grin at him all the while trying to steady the thumping in my chest. We enter the airport.

'There he is.' Gary nudges me and at the same time, he changes hands and carries his brief case in his left hand, leaving the right one free to shake hands with Nan.

Once out of the terminal and into the hot afternoon heat, he discards the board with our names on into the back of his vehicle. We toss our bags onto the seat and climb aboard ourselves. Chatting easily, we leave the airport and make our way, through countless streets thronging with people back to Nan's house.

We spend a pleasant evening with Nan and his wife and then after dinner get down to business in his den. Nan does not fit into the 'A Team' genre. His long lanky frame gives him an uncoordinated look, his thick dark hair is swept up in a pompadour hairstyle and he appears to be even taller than I had first thought. Nan is an amiable host, pouring a whiskey on the rocks for Gary and a cup of coffee for me, before settling back into his leather chair. We open the battered old leather brief case and remove our folder with proud panache. Laying the plans out onto the shiny mahogany coffee table, I hold my breath as he leans over frowning slightly, pursing his lips and concentrating as he has a look. The silence lengthens. He is suitably impressed, asking Gary many questions which they proceed to

151

discuss at some length. I nudge Gary with my foot and give him a clandestine thumb up sign. Things are going smoothly and we both feel confident and relaxed. We will soon be farming ostriches on this gorgeous sun kissed island. He mentions that the land he owns is not large, but he can lease more land if needed. He asks about our farm and we proudly show him a few photographs.

'5 000 acres Gary,' he grins 'that is some farm.' His eyebrows twitch dramatically.

Gary answers more questions about what we produce and we soon realise that Nan is not that knowledgeable about farming. We both smile at him as he unfolds, stretching his long frame.

'Excuse me. I will be back in a moment.' He leaves the room, closing the door with a gentle thud. The loud ticking from the clock on the wall accentuates the silence in the room. I finish the dregs of my coffee. A strong roasted aroma of percolated coffee floats in the air. Catching Gary's eye, he shrugs his shoulders and I realise that he is feeling tense. We so badly want this to work. We hear a scuffle outside the door and turn to look enquiringly at Nan as he enters. He offers more refreshments and on our refusal, folds his lanky frame back down onto his comfortable rust coloured leather chair, tapping the arm with long lean fingers. He casually mentions that he has organised a limo for us to use for our weeks stay, and carries on chatting, oblivious to the eye contact between Gary and I.

'A limo.' I mouth at Gary. He shrugs, the small frown creasing deeply between his dark eyebrows. Nan drops us off at the hotel and arranges to pick us up at nine sharp the following morning.

'A limo, Gary, what the hell is he on about? I hope we don't have to pay for it.' I give Gary a quizzical look. He is as puzzled about it as I am. Deciding that we will see what tomorrow brings, he pours us a drink from the bar we both gravitate to the French doors leading outside.

We sit on the small veranda of our hotel room overlooking the sea. I am entranced, as the light of the moon casts a gorgeous pale glow that glides serenely on the water. A million shimmering sensations spray high, silvery and magical. With our fingers entwined, relaxed and at ease for the first time in months, we watch the white horses dancing and cavorting on the crest of the waves. The salty smell of the ocean wafts over us, and the scenery makes the perfect backdrop for the hypnotic echo of the waves crashing in onto the beach.

'Well, Gary, as loath as I am to go inside, I feel as if I have tiny little weights sitting on my eye lashes; they keep making my eyelids close. I am absolutely bushed, and tomorrow will reveal all.' My smile is huge. 'Any more relaxed and I will be horizontal.'

'I can't wait to see what is in store for us tomorrow. I think Nan seems to be a genuine guy. What do you think?' He tilts his head to one side, looking at me with question mark eyebrows.

'He seemed to be impressed with your farming knowledge. Not that I think he is a connoisseur on farming. You could have baffled his brains with bullshit, and I don't think he would have been any the wiser.' With wonderful thoughts of living on this exotic island filling my mind, I pop my head down on the pillow and drift off into the moving stream of dreams.

I wake with the sunshine winking at me through the lace curtain, and nudging Gary with my elbow, he opens his eyes looking sleepy.

'Come on, Gary, let's get going. I want to go down to the beach.' We leap out of bed, pulling on our clothes, smoothing out the

153

typical suitcase creases. Locking the door behind us, he grabs my hand and we stroll down towards the sea. The sun is casting a golden shadow over the beach. Fingers of warmth reach out softly caressing my skin; I wiggle my toes in the soft sand, laughing as it sifts over my feet, tickling gently.

'What a start to the day.' I pull him up and run down to the water's edge. After a paddle in the warm inviting water, we sit out enjoying some fruit juice and warm buttered rolls, fresh out the oven this morning or so the waiter tells us. I stretch my legs, enjoying the warmth on my feet.

'This could all be ours hey, Gary.' I sweep my arm expansively, sighing deeply. 'The dogs could run on the beach, and Mikaela and Ben could come for holidays. Mum and dad, well, we will think on that one. I am sure there is something that they could do here.'

'Let's see the promised land first, Jen, before we get carried away on ocean madness.' He laughs at me.

We are both refreshed and looking forward to our first viewing of this beautiful island. Nan is bang on time and after a cheerful greeting we climb into his twin cab truck. After buckling ourselves in, he takes off, and I sit back, excited to see whether this could be the beginning of a new and wonderful world for us. Turning inland, I stare out the window, shattered when the gorgeous coastal glory turn into a slovenly pit hole of poverty. Nan chats away, oblivious to the poverty as we weave in and out of traffic, narrowly missing cyclists, mini buses, mangy looking dogs, and thin children playing perilously close to the speeding vehicles. I sit in the back clenching my butt muscles, wiping my sweaty hands and pushing my feet against imaginary breaks. I keep willing Nan to concentrate more and not turn around to talk to me.

He changes gear, doing a sharp turn with brakes squealing, as he eases the twin cab through a couple of banana trees. Inching forward slowly, we come to a halt in front of a tiny derelict cottage with a tin roof. I am holding my breath. Climbing out the twin cab and looking around, I close my mouth which had gaped open. Several mangy looking dogs, with long thread bare tails and fly eaten ears come slinking out of the shadows showing their teeth and growling, before being firmly admonished by Nan. Through a swirl of red dust and heat waves I view the scene.

What lies before us is about two acres of hard, sun baked earth, a derelict cottage, a few banana trees and not much more. The small cottage looks sad and neglected. A meter of brown hem, stained by water and mud splashes streaks the white washed exterior walls all the way around the cottage. A dirty tribute to the tropical rains that hiss and fight through the island. The windows are dressed in inches of grime and sealed with intricate cob webs that sway gently as I blow lightly on them. A couple of the panes are cracked adding artistic texture behind the cobweb curtain while others are broken. There is nothing welcoming about this sad little house: even given the fact that all it needs is a face lift.

I side step over a large crack and shudder as I am convinced, that little tail I caught sight of belongs to a scorpion. We climb back down the six steps, treading carefully over the white lumps of chicken shit that decorate the veranda and steps. The strong smell of ammonia stings my nostrils, and I glance at Gary raising my eyebrows enquiringly. He ignores me and keeps abreast of Nan as we stroll around the back of the cottage, nodding as he proudly points at a dozen free range chickens. A haze of little midges keep them busy as they scratch and peck at dry looking tufts of grass; a brave attempt at growth on the hard ground under a banana tree. A feeling of disbelief and disappointment hits me in the pit of my stomach. Our plan for ostrich farming needs a good five hundred acres, not two. There is nothing else to show us and we retreat to the veranda off the small cottage. After chasing the snarling dogs away again, he finds some old plastic bags in the back of his vehicle. We lay these on the steps and I sit down gingerly, careful not to get any of the grime on our clothes.

Gary has his brief case on his lap and he clicks the latch open. The lid remains closed, as we wait for Nan to start talking. I sit watching a colony of ants marching in perfect precision across the sun baked earth and I idly wonder if they are invasive or native. Nan's voice brings me back from my reverie and I prick up my ears.

'Gary, I can always find more land for you to lease, as I realise what we have here is not big enough.' He avoids any eye contact. I slide my eyes sideways, glancing at Gary and notice that he is frowning slightly, tapping his chin with a finger. Sitting under the harsh sun, the three of us get down to the nitty gritty of our business arrangement. I have this 'mad magazine' moment and can see the three of us in cartoon images sitting with our legs straight out in front of us, snarling dogs snapping at mine and Gary's feet. We hunch over, our long beak noses pecking at the words of an agreement, which has free range chicken shit dripping off it. I grin and shake my head to clear away the absurd picture. Our meeting takes no more than an hour, and it is becoming apparent that Nan's way of thinking has changed. He is holding back on us. We throw suggestions back and forth, and while he is excited about the whole project, he keeps insisting that we can find more land.

'Who will be financing this project?'

'Now we are talking, Gary.' Nan pushes his cap back off his forehead and scratches his head 'I will find more land for you,' and with my heart sinking I realise that Nan thinks that we will be putting up the finance.

'But, that is not what we were told when we went for the interview in Harare, Nan,' Gary's voice is low, tinged with disappointment.

'We don't have that sort of money, Nan.' I chip in.

'But what about your farm in Zimbabwe, Gary? You own 5 000 acres. You will be paid for that.' Nan's voice sounds avaricious. His dark eyes take on a guarded look as they slide from Gary to me, hiding behind a mask; I can feel the quiet.

'Nan, if I was going to be paid for my farm in Zimbabwe, I would not be looking for a job.' Gary sounds terse but Nan has an expression of disbelief on his face.

I feel that greed has poisoned the air. We sit for another half an hour before Nan is half convinced that we do not have the money. Something has changed since last night, and we could only think that it was the pictures of the farm. Land is at a premium price in Mauritius and we own five thousand acres in Zimbabwe. He is convinced that we have gold lined pockets.

We return to the hotel with a thoughtful and rather heavy silence pervading the vehicle. Nan buys us a cold beer and we all three sit, deep in our own thoughts before he again tries to convince us to part with money that we do not have. He is agitated and the pompadour hairstyle has lost its smooth slick look: his long fringe keeps flopping over one eye irritating the thick dark lashes, and he eventually gives in and pushes his cap back on to control his unruly hair.

'Would you excuse me for a couple of minutes? I just need to make a phone call.' We nod in unison at him.

We sit, drowsy with the beer and heat waiting for him to return. Gary leans over rubbing my bare arm gently, but says nothing.

Nan returns with long strides. 'I am sorry, but the limousine is no longer available.' His eyes dart from Gary's face to mine. I give him a high voltage stare and he looks down. 'There was a mistake on the booking for the car. It was double booked.' He digs the hole a bit deeper.

Gary kicks me under the table and I scowl at him, before having to bend down massaging my shin bone gently. I know he has seen me glare at Nan. We are not fools, naive yes, but not fools and he is lying to us. One morning in Mauritius and our plans for relocating are fast disappearing. Gary plays Nan at his own game and gives it one last attempt to convince him on the validity of our proposed project, but to no avail. He has closed his ears.

Nan waives us goodbye with a promise of picking us up in a week to take us back to the airport. As he makes a quick getaway, I turn to Gary.

'What the hell happened? Do you think he will pick us up in a week?' My voice is thick with emotion.

'Yes, Jen, he will pick us up. I think we have been taken for a couple of clients, Jen. I don't think these two business partners have the money to finance this project. Oh shit, I don't know' Gary shakes his head and we stand together, watching the twin cab disappear down the road and out of sight. 'Last night, when he thought we were rich, he was obviously chocolate farming. Stupid bugger went out to organise a limo for us, thinking we are rich.'

'He's taking our dream with him, Gary.' I feel close to tears. 'He is a stupid bloody dream thief.' We had put such a lot of research and work into the proposed project. I kick a stone in frustration, listening as it skids across the earth before coming to a standstill. 'This is how I am feeling; at a standstill and a total loss.' We have been banking on this job, and I had been swept away on a gold studded dream having seen the gorgeous sun kissed beach and aquamarine water.

We still have a week to get through and after a long walk along the beach, we sit lost in thought watching the surf. Lying back onto my elbows on the warm sand, I listen. The roar of the waves reaches a crescendo, before crashing in, white foam exploding from the force and racing up the beach towards my bare feet. This melody is interspersed with noisy squawks from the squabbling seagulls.

Nan, true to his word picks us up a week later and gives it one last crack to get us to part with money we do not have. I sit silently in the back of the twin cab listening to him wheedling. This is a good sales pitch, if ever I have heard one.

'Oh shut up, Nan. You are a real pain the arse.' I mutter quietly under my breath.

As the airport comes into view, I feel a sense of relief. We are going home. Nan's twin cab screeches to a halt outside a sign for Departures and we both jump out, thanking him for dropping us off.

'You know where I am if you change your mind, Gary.' and waving a hand he is gone. The last view I have of him, is with the wind from the open window gently lifting the gelled pompadour hairstyle, and turning to Gary, I grin.

'It has been a surreal week.' He nods at me, taking my arm. 'And we still have this amazing project, all ready and waiting. Somebody might want to take it on.

We buckle ourselves into our seat belts, and I take a deep breath as the plane revs up for takeoff. Once we reach altitude, and the plane has stopped shuddering, I unclip my belt and rub my neck trying to relax. Apart from the noise of the engine, there is a feeling of peace as we cruise the empty air spaces. I stare out the window, mesmerised by the clouds as they hang, light and diaphanous; scattering in the wind, losing their form and dissipating. The pilot announces that we are now flying over Zimbabwe. I peer through the mist of clouds. From the air, the country's commercial farms look deceptively peaceful. I gaze down at dams, streams, green pastures and cattle grazing. There are also some fields of healthy looking crops.

I sigh. 'I feel older and wiser and realise that we are so desperate for a job, that maybe we had only heard what we had wanted to hear at our interview in Harare. We will certainly not fall prey to anymore 'businessmen and their offers.'

I will also need to put out my 'dream catcher' again. There has to be something wonderful out there for us.

Chapter 24

OPERATION CHICKEN SANDWICH

After selling all the cattle, we have opened an off shore account and banked some American dollars or what we call real money. A perpetual grinding in our stomachs keeps reminding us that all our funds are tied up in the farm. We had, on one of our holidays down to South Africa bought a 'home course' on starting your own export business. Over the last year we have been doing just that. We found a contact in the UK by the name of Sally, sent her samples of cloth work; wooden carvings, soap stone statues and other oddments that we thought would be of interest to her. This was the start of G & J Enterprises. All products that Sally orders are then packed into crates and shipped over to the UK.

We spend hours exploring the markets in Harare, and over the last year we have got to know the talented artists that we deal with. I love nothing better than walking up and down the rows upon rows of artwork in the markets. Dust and flies swirls around your face, and the smell from the wood fires permeates your nostrils, clinging to your clothes and hair. I chuckle as I look around.

'Oh, Gary, I love Zimbabwe. What a rich life we have here. Even with all our problems, we are lucky.' I wave my hand expansively. 'Look at this. The talent of these people, the sun, and yes, even the bloody flies. I feel very passionate about our country.' I hug the fuzzy feeling that this sunburnt country in a small corner of the world arouses in me. 'Gary, I don't get any feeling of resentment from these people. The war vets on the farm are different, with their hatred and anger. These people here,' I spin around, 'they just want to make some money, and have law and order restored. They are all hard working citizens.' He takes my hand, squeezing tight.

The humanity that spills through the stalls is noisy, garish and African. We join the throngs of people, looking, laughing and discovering treasures. Canvases, ablaze with colour, beckon those with a passion for painting. This rough, open air gallery pulsates with movement; vivid stories unfolding onto the canvases, depicting nature, life and the courage of the human spirit. The smoke from the wood fires curl upwards, catching the breeze, fluttering softly before dispersing. The open fire is the only means these people have for cooking. A delicious smell of 'roasted mealies'; maize cobs suspended by a kebab stick over the hot coals awaken your senses, making your taste buds groan in anticipation. This smoky flavour from the open coals turns a plain maize cob into a 'cob deluxe.'

I wander between these basic structures marvelling at the sights and smells. The small children scuttle out of my way, and peer at me from under rickety tables with their big solemn brown eyes, before giving a delightful grin, teeth white against their dark skin. Our Zimbabwean carvers are renowned for their natural talent, which is found in their work. I stop, enthralled and spend ages standing, arms folded and leaning comfortably against a table watching a carver working. He chips away at a chunk of wood. Using the most basic tools, he carves an amazing replica of an elephant, hippo or other wild animal.

'You buy. Very cheap.' The carver stops work, picks up a small carving and holds out his hand. A small elephant, about six inches by six inches, treads softly over his palm towards me. I take it, caressing the smooth shiny body, staring into the small eye, full of life and expression.

'It is beautiful. How much is it? Have you only got one?' I ask.

He leans backwards, stretching his lean arm out to the side of him, pulling a plastic crate towards me.

162

'I have a herd. You want all.' He entices me to look. We haggle noisily, before agreeing on a price. He wraps my family of six elephant in newspaper, tucking them into an old plastic bag. I pay him.

'Thank you. They are beautiful.' I repeat, totally enchanted with the herd of elephant that evoke strong emotions as sweet as the breath of a warm wind. Turning away, my eyes scan the crowd looking for Gary.

'Look, I have bought a whole herd. I think we may have discovered a new carver here, Gary.' I unwrap one, laughing as the paper unfurls as delicately as the frond of a fern, ready to uncover the secret of a new life. The carving ambles from my palm onto his, and I point out the guy, who is watching our reaction with a crooked grin. Gary walks over to his stall and I turn away as he becomes engrossed in discovering more treasures. The dust closes around him like a gauzy curtain.

No two carvings are ever the same. Some work is sandpapered, giving a smooth and polished look and feel. Others are delicately etched, giving texture and roughness. I am totally enthralled with the hours we spend in these market places. Carved animals, like sentinels guard the front of the stalls. Wooden spoons, bowls, ashtrays, beads and other oddments clutter the counters. Long thin fingers, disappear into mysterious folds in pockets, picking out change and tucking notes back into safety, out of view from would be thieves. The vendors love to haggle, attracting the attention of others. We stand, surrounded by curious onlookers, nudging, laughing and encouraging a higher price as we come to an arrangement on our purchases; paying out notes that are then folded and tucked away into obscurity.

'No I am very sorry. I don't want to buy it.' I cringe inside, as his thin shoulders slump and his eyes take on a haunted look. He pushes it towards me. The piece of sculpture is modern, smooth and full of curves, but it is not what we are looking for. I shake my head. He continues to beg, and I walk away.

Looking around the market 90% of these people are thin, tired and wearing clothes that are faded, patched and torn through constant wear. Scuffed shoes adorn adult feet and children are more often than not barefoot. Their small wide feet and rough heels leave a myriad of foot prints on the ground, disturbing the sand between the roughly erected wooden stalls. Babies are kept on the backs of their mothers, bound securely with a large bath towel or long strip of fabric. Any crying is negated by a jiggling up and down motion or one arm folding up and behind to pat the small bundle on the bum. The constant movement by the mother lulls the babes into contented sleep, oblivious of the impending hardship coming their way.

Batiks and other cloth work flap in the breeze, grazing your cheek gently as you duck, avoiding the over head wire adorned with wind chimers, all swaying and tinkling.

The political situation in Zimbabwe is affecting all citizens; sadly a knock on effect from the farm invasions and chaos. These people rely on trade from the tourists, which are fast diminishing, and turning their eyes to more peaceful holiday surroundings. However, these people at the markets are always cheerful and desperate for business. The low buzz of laughter and conversation makes for the perfect union with the static sound of music blaring from the odd battery run radio, and the shrill shrieks of children. We visit this market place often, buying what we can for export.

I have been producing a lot of wildlife paintings and selling some locally. The majority of my work gets taken down to my brother

Ken in South Africa. He owns a pub in Johannesburg, and sells my work through the pub. We pack the back of the pickup up with ten or so paintings, all mounted and framed and cover them with a blanket. I wrap a couple of paintings in brightly coloured birthday paper and leave these in view on top of the blanket. We also deal in lamps made of plastic pipe, and elaborately carved with African wildlife. These do not look like anything special until lit. The light shines through the carved areas, and these lamps take on a life of their own; a scene so alive and mellow with the soft glow throwing shadows onto the walls. Most of these lamps are packed in boxes and hidden under the blanket. Some, we leave on top with the suitcase and the wrapped paintings. Around the lamps and my pictures, we pack in a few of the carvings and other oddments that we have found at the market.

With the truck all packed up, we leave the farm and drive the twelve hour journey to Johannesburg. The long journey takes us through Masvingo, and we stop at Rileys Garage, hoping that they will have fuel to top us up. It will save us spending our much needed foreign currency. Gary catches me rubbing my stomach which gurgles like a noisy water pipe and so we decide to have a quick bite at the Wimpy restaurant. We slide into the bench seats and look at the menu. The pleasant waitress wearing a wide smile pads towards our table, her smooth plump arms swinging loosely by her rotund waist. She is a vision of health as she leans over, her buxom boobs fighting for freedom. We are the only customers.

'Good morning.' She croons huskily.

'Good morning.' We both answer in unison.

'I would like a toasted cheese and tomato sandwich, chips and a cup of coffee please.' Gary smiles at her.

'I am sorry Sir, but we don't have any cheese.' She is apologetic.

'You have got to be joking!' Gary's reaction is immediate and his tone is cutting. I kick him under the table.

'Cool it Gary. For goodness sake it's only cheese,' I feel annoyed that he should get so edgy about cheese.

'Ok, I will have toasted bacon and egg sandwich please.' He raises his eyebrows, waiting, and she trots off to confirm whether they have bacon. I take the opportunity to voice my irritation.

'What the hell is wrong with you Gary? It's just a sandwich, and she is just the waitress.' I trail off as she comes back, confirming that there is bacon. She then turns to me.

'I would like a tomato sandwich and a diet coke please,' I look up at her, flashing my best smile.

She rolls her eyes and shakes her head sadly 'I am sorry but we don't have any diet coke.'

'No bloody diet coke. I don't believe it. A wimpy restaurant, and there is no diet coke!' I am fizzing. A sharp and painful thud on my shin stops my rant and I look over the table at Gary, who is grinning. 'Ouch, that was bloody sore, Gary.'

'It is only a diet coke.' He widens his eyes at me, and the waitress studiously studies her nails, impervious to the small domestic taking place.

I decide on a cup of coffee and crinkle my nose at him over the table as a giggle bursts forth making him laugh. He takes my hand over the table, caressing my wrist with his thumb. It is good to laugh. Our breakfast duly arrives, and it is delicious, even though I have had to wash it down with strong coffee served in a thick rimmed cup.

'Why are we making a fuss? Cheese and diet coke are the least important issues in our life. Come on, let's go. We need to get across the border, and we can have all the cheese and all the diet coke we want.' We ask for the bill, tipping the waitress before braving the toilets and leaving.

The tar road is in surprisingly good condition, and we pick up speed as there is little traffic. We stop again at the Lion and Elephant Motel, where they do have diet coke. Another quick toilet break and we are back on the road leaving us with an hours' drive to reach the border post. We cross the dry, sandy Bubi River, slowing down as the goats amble along the grassy verge, lawn mowers on four legs as they gobble everything in sight. They are a menace to vehicles travelling this stretch of road.

'There she is, Gary. Come on pull off.' I am pointing towards the macabre giant looming in the distance. 'I won't take long.'

Indicating left, we pull off onto the dirt, taking a minute or two to stare in awe at the huge baobab tree with its' magnificent girth. The smaller scrubby bushes stare up in awe, as the wind carries whispers of angry gods teaching the baobab trees a lesson by tearing them from the harsh earth and re-planting them upside down.

'Its branches sway like crooked limbs.' I raise my arms, 'I love this tree. Its scrubby neighbours look so insignificant living next door to this beauty.'

'It's a beauty alright. It could be one of the biggest in Zim. I am not sure'. He smiles. The neglected building at the border post comes into view. My heart starts bouncing about, on the loose and out of control. My mouth feels so dry, that the inner folds of my cheeks are glued to my teeth. We stand in a long queue, waiting patiently for our turn to have our passports stamped. Back out in the heat, I take a deep breath. We are nearly over the first hurdle of our journey. As the

Zimbabwean official drops the boom behind us, I take another big breath. Driving slowing over the bridge, the South African customs buildings look fresh and once again my heart goes on the rampage.

'Now we need to get through the boom on the South African side.' He raises his eyebrows.

Our passports and the official looking forms with 'nothing to declare' on are soon stamped. Now! We need to get through the boom. We have however, learnt a trick or two, and leave a few chicken sandwiches, with mayonnaise on the dashboard. The spicy smell of fried chicken mingles with the aroma of fresh bread, teasing and tantalising the taste buds. These cannot be taken through the border post. As we pull up to the boom I open my window, and the over plump African gent leans his head through to talk. I watch his huge nostrils dilate. The thick nose hairs quiver as his pink tongue darts out tasting the air and he licks his full lips. His eyes flash around the cab looking for the source of the aroma. The customs official pounces on the sandwiches clearing his throat.

'I am sorry but you are not allowed to take meat through the border post. You will have to throw it away.' I can hear him swallowing his saliva. This is better than I had hoped. I pucker my lips, looking sad.

'Oh no, are you sure? Would you like it as it seems a terrible waste to throw it away?' He is drooling as his pudgy fingers close over the grease proof wrapped sandwich.

'Yes, thank you very much.' His polite answer has my insides bubbling over with humour, tinged with nerves. We chat for a second or two and I watch with a 'mournful look' as he retreats to his small wooden shack, his large posterior shaking and shuddering; rather like two pigs cavorting under a blanket. I know he cannot wait to sink his teeth into the sandwich. This has certainly got his mind off looking in the back, and he opens the boom munching greedily on our delicious sandwich as he waves us through. The heavy boom slams down with a loud decisive clunk, and I turn to Gary with a mischievous grin plastered on my face.

'Operation chicken sandwich has done it again.' I giggle nervously and feel a sense of freedom. This little trick works every time and it is all part of our 'survival strategy.' The soft soothing tone of Bob Marley's song three little birds fills the car, and leaning over I turn it up, looking towards Gary and singing along, 'don't worry about a thing, cause every little thing gonna be all right.' I tap along to the music, 'saying, this is my message to you-ou-ou.'

'What an appropriate song to be singing when we have just smuggled your paintings, US dollars and other goods through the border customs. I won't worry about a thing, cause every little thing gonna be all right.' He sings along with me. We make our way to Johannesburg, our rendezvous with my brother Ken, and it's all about topping up the coffers. We spend four pleasant and relaxing nights with Ken before it is time to say goodbye and we are once again on the road.

Travelling back through the border post poses no problem, and we are soon home on the farm, neck deep in tension.

The Government is making it so difficult for us to live a normal existence. It is illegal to be in possession of, and to be dealing in foreign currency. The banks are short of US dollars and even then, dealing with them, we will get a pittance of an exchange rate. Some fat cat from the bank will deal on the black market and make a fortune. The government is at this stage, offering rewards for people to turn in acquaintances, friends and family who are dealing illegally in foreign currency.

We have a briefcase full of Zimbabwe dollars and we are desperate for US dollars. A year or so previously Gary had spoken to an Asian contact about marketing Rhodes grass seed. Over a period of months they had got to know each other over the phone, but have never met in person. Trying to rid ourselves of our briefcase full of cash, we make telephone contact with an Asian man whose number we have been given. It just so happens to be the same man that Gary has spoken to on many previous occasions re the Rhodes grass seed that we export.

Gary and I go through to Harare to meet up with him. They had both decided to meet at a mutual venue in the Industrial sites. I am feeling anxious. We know that what we are doing is illegal, adding to the excitement and increased heart rate. We sit waiting, watchful and alert. Eventually a twin cab with darkened windows cruises past and disappears behind one of the large shipping containers. Gary picks up his briefcase and after closing the door gently behind him, he slides furtively after the twin cab. Five minutes have already gone past. I can feel the quiet; interspersed by the rhythmic tattoo of my fingers on the dashboard. I know that it will be taking a long time to count out the Zimbabwe dollars. My neck feels tight, my muscles squealing as I keep watch in the side mirror; looking for imaginary witnesses to our illegal dealings. Waiting is hard, and I try hard to ignore my mind.

After what seems to be an eternity Gary appears, trying to look casual, as he strolls nonchalantly toward the truck, his feet kicking up small puffs of dust. I have already climbed into the driver's seat and have the engine running by the time he opens the passenger door. We leave the premises as quickly and unobtrusively as we can.

'Well no one could ever say living in Zimbabwe is boring hey? What do you think?' I light up a cigarette spluttering, laughing and coughing at the same time.

'No most certainly not boring Jen. Only problem now is we have a whole lot of US dollars that need to be smuggled out the country.' Gary has narrowed his eyes, a guard against the cigarette smoke.

'Oh damn. I had forgotten about that. So what's next; Operation Chicken Sandwich again. I don't know if my nerves can take this Gary.' I close my eyes dramatically and enjoy the last puff on the cigarette.

At least G & J Enterprises can move with us when we leave the farm and we can still continue to reap the benefits from our export business.

Chapter 25

THE GOVERNMENT VALUATOR'S TAPE MEASURE

The daily problems facing our survival on the farm are being tested to the limit. We had been presented with a section 8 from the government a couple of months ago. (A section 8 is an order from the government to vacate the farm within 30 days). It had occurred just before Maggie died. We know we are going to have to vacate the farm. It is just a matter of when.

'Gary, I had so hoped that they were going to let us finish the season?' Dad's face shows the weary lines of strain that is beginning to take a toll. He knows deep down that his and mums' retirement plans are back onto the drawing board. However, he is trying to be optimistic.

'Dad, from the moment they stopped us from watering the tobacco seedbeds, but allowed us to continue ploughing the lands, I suspected something more sinister was up. Now, I know they wanted some land prep done for them. As soon as they started planting maize in the lands that we had ploughed, I have accepted that we are out.' Gary rubs his face, shaking his head. 'I suppose we have been hanging in for as long as we could. Hope always springs eternal.'

'What are all these people going to do?' Mum asks. 'I feel so sorry for them. Dad and I passed a couple of women with their meagre bundles of clothes trudging up the road. A small girl was struggling behind them, carrying a large plastic dish. It was a sorry sight.'

'The knock on effect of these farm invasions is huge. I don't know how many African people are employed on the farms

172

countrywide, but it is going to become a human tragedy. A percentage of these people have no homelands to go to.' Gary lights a cigarette, dragging deeply. 'We have tried so hard to avoid what is now going to happen. My heart feels like it is going to break. Thank goodness, I have an interview with Mike.' We are both banking on him getting this job growing flowers for export. 'I hate having to drive past the lands with the dead vegetable plants, the seedbeds and when I see houses in my ploughed lands, it does my head in. I have worked my whole adult life to achieve all this, and poof,' he snaps his fingers, 'it is gone.'

The war vets have felt the shift of power and are pulling no punches now. They want us off the land, and quickly. Over the last eighteen months we have tried to keep our heads down. The farm invasions have felt like an unrehearsed nightmare and we are exhausted. Mugabe is determined to stay in power at the cost of the agricultural sector and the knock on effect from this will eventually corrode into every other business on a national basis. No one will be safe from him.

I am elbow deep in soil as Adam and I are potting some of my more precious plants; plants that have made the trek with us over the years. They feed my soul, and will continue to do so when we move. A shaft of sunshine, as delicate as spiders silk thread weaves through the afternoon shade, catching my eye; and hence, catching my breath. I look at what we have built and my heart is heavy. My tears are only water and I know that, even though my heart is breaking, given time it will become whole again. We will survive. A light breeze ruffles my hair; I clutch at it, holding it close to my cheek. Maggie, I think is near. I often feel her presence and it calms my disorientated thoughts.

Adam is gently removing plants from the ground, taking care not to damage their intricate root system before re-potting, either into a large fertilizer bags or large ceramic pots. I am determined to take as many plants as I can. The smell of damp soil, earthy and slightly pongy entices the dogs to join us. They are scratching and digging in the flower bed. I chase them out for the umpteenth time, laughing as they make their escape. Toffee has managed to remove a chunk of day lily and Beano gives chase trying to wrestle it from her mouth. Barking excitedly and managing to get her teeth around the roots, they pursue a tug of war game. I smile like an indulgent mother before turning back to the task at hand. Adam is loading the bags onto the wheel barrow, arm muscles taut as he grunts with exertion. I know the garden is going to die over the following year, but I dare not let my mind go there.

'Ndiani?' (Who is that?) Adam asks me as he points towards the small gate leading to the workshop area. A young African man is leaning on the gate, long arms dangling over, watching us.

'Masikati.' (Good afternoon) I greet him as I walk slowly towards the small gate, wiping my dirty hands down my trouser clad thighs. I have never seen him before and am suspicious of any strangers. The dogs look up, dropping their tug of war game and come running from the long shadows behind the house, barking. The young man leaps back from the gate, hastily popping his hands into the safety of his pockets. He greets me back and I turn as Adam's shadow falls over me. They start to speak in Shona. I listen, picking up a word here and there. Damn, I knew I should have insisted on Maggie teaching me the language.

Adam turns to me 'Boss ari kupi?' (Where is the boss?) I tell him that I will go and find him.

Gary follows me out wearing a small frown. The afternoon shadows cower from the heat, and I can feel the dampness prickling under my hairline. The closeness of the heat has done nothing to dampen the young African man's rather forceful manner or the strong pungent smell escaping his armpits. He has had a long walk and a fine dust has settled on his short curly hair giving him a premature grey look.

'What is it you want?' Gary's voice is terse, but pleasant. 'Have you any paper work or identification?'

'Here you are. I have come from the local farm school.' This school is situated on a farm a couple of kilometres away. He hands over his ID card, mindful of the dogs. 'I have come to do a valuation on this farm. I am a school teacher, but today, I am the Government valuator. My job is to come here today.'

'You are the Government valuator?' Well what do you know?' Gary's tone turns icy. He reaches into his pocket, lighting a cigarette. I know he is trying to calm himself. 'And, you a school teacher?' The young man nods. 'This farm is huge, and you have come to do a valuation on foot. Interesting!' He coughs, staring the young man straight in the eye. 'How are you going to measure the fencing?' Gary's voice raises a couple of octaves. I lean over, putting my hand on his forearm, squeezing gently, trying to keep his manner calm.

'I will do what I can do.' The young man stutters.

Within a few minutes of talking to him, we realize that he is just not qualified to do a valuation on our farm. The government are really pulling a fast one now. His thin arms stick out of large cropped sleeves and hang awkwardly by his sides, his long fingers fidgeting. A small pad and pencil peep out of his top pocket. Khaki trousers hang loosely over his long legs, stopping slightly short of his ankles, allowing a glimpse of black socks sporting Homer Simpson's rather comical face in bright yellow, before disappearing into scuffed brown lace up shoes.

175

'Well, I suggest you make a start then.' Gary is frustrated and I don't blame him. However, this will not get us anywhere. He stands foursquare; his arms folded staring with irritation at the intruder.

His rather cocky demeanour changes; our welcome has been cool. Our farm is five thousand acres and one of his first jobs would be to measure the fencing, forty two kilometres of it. The young man removes the small pad and pencil from his top pocket and I can see that his long and expressive fingers are shaking. He is totally unsure on how to proceed. We all stand watching each other, feeling awkward, before, with a pathetic whine in his voice he asks if he can come into the house.

We open the gate and he follows us to the back door. Edna is in the ironing room. She opens the door to see what the ruckus is all about, as like us, she is suspicious of strangers. Her dark brown eyes flash to mine. I smile, reassuring her that all is well, and she closes the door again. He loiters in the doorway to the kitchen and with an impatient gesture I invite him in. I am irritated to have this man invading our space, but to have an incompetent one ruining our limited time left on the farm is like an insult. He stands, dark eyes taking in kitchen cupboards, stove, washing up sinks etc. His one hand is clutching the pen and pad, while the index finger on his other hand rubs up and down his broad nose. He does not dare to open any kitchen cupboards, and I mutter impatiently under my breath. He asks if he can see the bathroom, suddenly unsure of himself. He follows me down the passage, stopping at every bedroom doorway, not entering but feasting his eyes on all our personal property and recording nothing in the notepad. Gary pads, like an agitated cat behind us and if he had a tail, it would be swishing back and forth. He is having a job controlling his irritation.

The bathroom is tastefully done in pale pink marbled tiles, all laid by Adam, Gary and myself. In the large mirror on the side of the

176

bath I stare at Gary's reflection as he leans against the far wall, the furrows between his eyebrows deep, as he shakes his head. Our eyes meet and he shrugs his shoulders. The Government valuator puts his hand into his pocket and pulls out a dirty tattered old tape measure, its edges worn and fraying. He screws up his eyes as he peers at the faded numbers. It looks as if it has been discovered in an ancient sewing basket. We both stand transfixed as he proceeds to measure the height of the basin, slowly and methodically, recording his results in the little notebook. With a solemn look, and much lip nibbling, he informs us that he has now finished. The look of total disbelief on Gary's face is priceless. I feel a pressure building in my stomach, and I desperately try to control the hysterical laughter that is threatening to erupt. Hunching my shoulders up under my ears, I wrestle with the urge to burst, biting my lip as I watch the young man measure and re-measure the basin four times. Gary and I follow him back down the passage and through the kitchen to the back door. This is the only measurement that is taken and recorded; our farm's value is going to be calculated on the height of a wash basin.

As he walks back towards the work shop area and disappears through the gate, a strange sound; a cross between a wheeze and a guffaw erupts from my mouth and the two of us stand with tears running down our faces laughing hysterically.

'I wonder how valuable our basin will prove to be,' I clutch my stomach.

'Let's put it this way Jen. I don't think we will be able to cruise the world on that particular asset hey. Did that half hour really happen? Is this all really happening?' I stop laughing, staring at Gary.

'How lucky we have had an independent valuation done Jen. I can't see many bank notes coming our way from what has just happened.' He shakes his head.

'Hey Geerry dipa sweetie,' the harridan screeches as us, cackling loudly, her long thin arms hanging loosely over the gate. She knows that the valuator has just vacated the house. To ask for sweets just adds to the bizarre encounter.

'Bugger off you old witch. Go and find yourself a broom, and do us all a favour. Fly far away.' Gary retorts angrily waving a hand in the air, dismissing her. She turns on her heel, chortling loudly as she disappears around the corner of the workshop. She is a continual thorn in his side.

I scurry through the kitchen, popping on the kettle before I open the gate on the veranda grill. I stand watching Adam gently cradling plants before re-planting them. The valuator never did look around the farm. I catch sight of him trudging slowly up the steep hill. 'Binoculars.' I am talking to myself, as I run through to the bedroom, to find them. Peering out the bedroom window I focus the lenses on Homo Simpsons face on his socks 'Idiot man,' I mutter 'both of them.' I can see no sign of the little book. I would give my eye teeth to know what is going through his mind. I keep my eyes on him until he disappears like a small dot over the crest of the hill.

I make myself a cup of tea and sitting down on the steps of the veranda I look around the garden. My God, it is so beautiful here. Our little piece of paradise and we are going to lose it all. The hush of late afternoon settles over the garden. My thoughts run wild, and what had earlier been hysterical laughter, is now raw emotion. It explodes from my chest and I weep. When I next look up, Adam has disappeared. I am not sure how long I sit, hugging my melancholy. That silly little man has upset me. I miss Maggie. I try to remember when things had changed, and when our hope had been taken away. 'Get a grip,' I admonish myself. Locking the grill door I retreat to the bathroom for another look at the fascinating basin.

Chapter 26

A MEMORABLE BIRTHDAY 2001

I am excited as we are getting off the farm and going through to Harare for the day. It is Mikaela's birthday and we are going to spoil her with a delicious lunch. As we drive out through the workshop area, I cock my head to one side.

'What the hell is that noise all about Gary?' Loud chanting vibrates on the breeze. I turn to Gary, my eyes huge and enquiring as fear spreads through my body like a raging fire. Before I can say another word, they appear; these men wrapped in cloths of violence, arms raised, fists clenched and hatred blazing from their eyes. Jarent can be seen towards the back of the mob, his fist raised in anger. We are forced to stop as they close around the car, blocking out the sunshine. There are at least twenty of them, armed with their pipes, machetes and pick handles. The fear invades my senses, silent and menacing; it flanks me. The car seems to take on a life of its own, rocking back and forth, gently; then gathering momentum. I feel this pressure building up deep inside me.

'Gary, please do something.' I am sitting on my trembling hands. He pops his shoulder against the door, managing to push it open, trying to ignore the snarling faces snapping at him through the closed window. He stands with one leg outside, leaning with one elbow on the roof and the other on the open door. Desperate to get some sort of dialogue going, he tries to still his pounding heart. The menace, a thick cloying fog fills the car, snaking around my legs and I become fear. I watch as my heart appears to be pounding in my feet. A strong pungent odour drifts through the open window of the car and sliding my eyes sideways I am relieved to see that the men at my window are now talking to Gary over the roof. A trickle of perspiration slides down my back. I can feel that my cheeks are bright red and burning. It seems like forever until Gary climbs back into the car. He reverses back towards the gate.

'I have persuaded them to let you go back inside. Radio the Godfather and report this. I have got to go back and talk to them.' He tells me through clenched teeth, his jaw locked and rigid.

'Gary, watch your head.' I can hardly get the words out as my tongue feels thick and dry. 'Please be careful. I love you.' Climbing out of the car, and aware of yellow eyes boring into my back, I open the gate, walking until I am out of sight.

'Are you okay?' Adam's eyes are concerned.

'Adam, yes I am fine. I need to phone. Please just stand this side of the wall and listen. If they are going to hurt the boss, please run inside and tell me.' I run to the back door, grabbing a glass off the sink and filling it with water, as I have no spit left in my mouth. With my voice quavering, I report the incident to the Godfather.

'Jen, I will call a few guys on the task force. Give us an hour. Have they threatened Gary?'

'No, but there is a large angry mob at the workshop and I am frightened.'

'Listen, just keep an ear out. Any changes and we will be on our way. I will phone a couple of guys, but we need to see if this is going to escalate.'

'Thank you.' I look at my watch. Shit, an hour seems like an eternity. The shrill ringing interrupts my thoughts. I snatch up the phone.

'Jen, I overheard your conversation. What the hell is going on down there? Where is Gary?' Mum's voice is frantic.

'Mum, Gary is negotiating with them. They are angry as hell with us because we are still resident on the farm.' I lick my lips. 'Is dad there with you?'

'Yes, he is. We are going to come down.'

'No, for heaven's sake, Mum...' I swallow. 'No. Please will you and dad get into 'greasy dick' (their old Mercedes Benz) and go up to Kiki and Wynand (our neighbours). I want you to go now.'

'No, I am not leaving you.' She replies stubbornly. 'We are going to come down. We will come through the front gate.'

'Mum. No.' I am tense. 'Listen to me.' I sound stern. 'These people can get from the workshop to your gate quicker than the two of you can make it from the back door to your car. I am worrying about Gary at this present time, Mum, and I do not need to be worrying about you and Dad as well.'

'Well only if you are sure. I don't want to leave you both behind.'

'Mum, please just go now.' I reply. 'Just go now.' It is not long before I see their old orange Mercedes trundling slowly up the hill, cloud of dust trailing behind them. Breathing a sigh of relief I bend down patting the dogs before returning to the bathroom window. I listen with a pounding heart to the negotiations going on behind the garden wall. It is the longest hour of my life. Waiting, we always seem to be waiting. I realise that if we carry on like this, we will always be waiting for change, and it will never come. We will have to be the change; get on with our lives and stop waiting. Gary eventually trudges back into the house looking pale and weary. I radio the godfather, and phone mum and dad, who have been offered lunch at our neighbours. Thank goodness, feelings on the ground will have cooled down by the time they return.

'When is this ever going to end?' I ponder quietly as we leave by the front gate. 'That little scene out at the workshops has been a terrifying reminder on what our lives have become, Gary, and it is one that I don't care to repeat.'

'The war vets are seriously angry because we have showed no signs of leaving. They want us off the farm. We are in a predicament. As you know, we have spent huge amounts of money on the seedbeds and land preparation, and they are planting their bloody crops out into our prepared lands. This is our life, our home and our work. These buggers want it all, Jen. I just don't know anymore. What the hell are we going to do? They refuse to have any discussions about this. They do not want to involve the District Administrator (Government position), as they say it is not necessary as their power is greater.' Gary's face looks grey. He appears to have shrunk in the last hour.

'I...' I tail off, staring into the distance. I can't think straight.

'These guys are controlling us and I don't believe they will stop at anything to achieve what they want. I am tired now. They have worn me down, and I worry about you, and the folks.' His eyes are dull. His hand is shaking as it finds the scar on his forehead and he runs his finger along the jagged edge, remembering.

Our lunch with Mikaela is full of false cheer. She opens her card and present smiling gently at me. I hide behind my cheerful smile, prattling on and she looks at me, narrowing her eyes.

'What is going on?' I smile widely. 'No, Mum, don't do that. What has happened?' She bangs her hand on the table.

'We had a slight problem this morning. Dad managed to diffuse the situation, but oh, bloody hell, it was terrifying.' I screw my eyes tight, trying to stop the flow of tears, which squeeze through my lids, flowing down my cheeks. 'I am sorry. We did not want to spoil the lunch.' I recount the mornings' events, blowing my nose on the tissue that she has handed me. She shakes her head.

'Oh, Mum, I am so sorry.'

'I feel sad because I now realise that we are going to have to leave. I kept hoping some sanity would prevail. I now know that dad and I can't wait around for too much longer. We need to go and find our laughter again, because if we don't, we will end up like Maggie and that is too final for me.' It is a weak attempt at some humour.

Chapter 27

THE HARRIDON TAKES OVER

We have managed to find a house in Marondera that will be suitable for my Mum and Dad. Doug Whaley (a neighbour and friend) kindly lends us a lorry. Once the furniture is loaded, covered with a tarpaulin and secured down with ropes, we are ready to leave. It is a sad day for them. A day that rolls on with a grumble of thunder and the smell of anger hangs in the air.

Their time on the farm, though short lived has been, up until the last eighteen months blissful. Memories will be reeled up tight and unravelled when the hurt is less painful. Poor mum climbs into their old Mercedes tucking her skirt around her tired spider veined legs, her blue eyes roaming around the garden, holding onto her emotions. Losing your home is not easy and losing your home when you are in your middle seventies is extremely disorientating. Mum's heart has been shredded by the resident vultures, but it will mend.

'No, don't go yet.' She holds dad's arm. 'I just want to gather more images.' The tears roll down her cheeks. She looks up towards the gate where a contingent of war vets have collected, toy toying rhythmically and chanting loudly; throwing a farewell party. A couple of them are waving their hands dismissively, shouting comments. 'Ok, let's do this, and get it over with.' She blows all emotion into her tissue. I pat her arm.

'Love you Mum. We are survivors.' I whisper, crossing my fingers tight. 'Don't look at the woman, alright? I wish you had your catapult and a faster car.' She turns to me, and her blue eyes sparkle mischievously.

'I had my chance, but I blew it. I should have ambushed her with my catapult months ago. See you at the new house.' My heart swells at her bravado. Philly and Lulu are in the back of the car. Lulu grins, little hand giving me a cheerful wave as her short little plaits bob merrily. Oh the innocence of the young.

Mum stares straight ahead, holding a hand to her trembling lips as they drive through the gates for the last time. Dad's trilby is pulled down, hiding the shimmer in his eyes. Neither glance towards the woman who has caused such pain, but their greatest pain comes from having to leave and we all know that they will never return to the farm that had become their home. They drive away with dignity.

I follow closely behind the old Mercedes closing my window to the snarling women.

'Go fly away you witch.' I mutter. The swirling dust clogs my throat; stifling the emotion and keeps it lodged in my chest. I feel the tears stroking my cheeks and I lift a hand, wiping them away. The two small dogs are lying quietly in the floor well; wet little noses pressed tight under their front legs. Gary's truck is loaded up with plants. Anton (Philly's husband) sits in the front seat. He will be working with Gary at the flower farm. We make a sad little convoy leaving the farm.

We spend the day settling them in, unpacking boxes, hanging curtains and by the afternoon the bed is made, cupboards are full and the lounge chairs are positioned around the fire place. Outside the back door all the packing cases have been folded down and are being loaded back onto the lorry. We will reuse them for our move. My mind balks at the thought.

Going home is strange. The cottage lies in darkness. It frowns down on us as we pass. We have work to do, as we will be leaving the farm within the week. We have found a place to live outside

Marondera within a stone's throw of the Peterhouse High Schools. Gary has started a job growing flowers for Mike Bailey; a huge relief to know some money will be coming in again. The last four months had taken a toll on us and on our bank balance.

The following week is like working our way through cotton wool. We do our best to keep ourselves grounded. Gary has managed to find employment for a few of the farm labourers, and another handful has been signed on with him at the flower farm. All labourers have been paid their gratuities. The old geriatrics cast a sad shadow, their thin bodies hunched protectively against the outside world as they shuffle up the road, a small bundle of blankets and a couple of pots, their only load. We know that they are at least going back to their families where they will scratch a living in their barren homelands until they pass onto greener pastures. The problem of living back in the homelands is that they then fall under the control of the ZANU PF thugs, who sweep in and out of the small villages, pushing their weight around. Their control over these people is fuelled through fear. Jim, our main crop guard, shuffles his scuffed shoes in the dust as he hands his weapon back. Gary gives him a cap to replace his tatty, threadbare old hat. Jim cups his hands with appreciation at his gratuity pay, which he tucks away into his threadbare shorts. He has nowhere to go.

'Jim, why don't you find a bit of land on the farm?' Gary is sincere. This has been suggested to different members of the labour force and the answer is always the same.

'I think I am going to go back to Mozambique. I know there are maybe some jobs with farmers from Ruzawi (a neighbouring district) who are now farming in Mozambique.'

'Thank you.' Gary shakes his hand. 'Famba zvakanaka, Jim.' (Bon voyage, go well) Gary's eyes are as turbulent as stormy seas.

186

Jarent takes his gratuity without meeting Gary's eye. He tucks the folded notes away into his well worn pocket, and turns away. For ten years he has been driving our tractors and now it all does not seem to matter. Gary can't bring himself to say thank you any more than Jarent can. He has mutated over the past eighteen months into someone we do not know and I watch as the labour keep well away from him. He has helped to make their lives miserable since the farm occupations.

My heart bleeds and my soul mourns as I watch the disintegration of Methven Ranch's human side. There is a constant wave of human traffic flowing past our fence. Families trudge slowly past the fence before toiling up the steep road leading off the farm. Woman and girls are weighed down with bundles on their heads, forgetting about trying to push back the small dark springs of hair that have escaped from under their dooks. With their backs straighter than pins, neck muscles thickly roped and protesting against the load on their heads, they appear to glide, rather than walk. Girls as young as seven have babies tied securely to their backs with a bereka (towel tucked firmly around the body to hold a baby firmly on ones back). Smaller children, carrying lighter items toil along behind, their shorter legs peppered with dust. It is a hot and humid afternoon. Cumulus clouds burst up and over the horizon. I worry for these people on the move with all their worldly belongings on their person. Are they going to get caught in a down pour? The farm could do with some rain. 'Absurd thought.' I mutter, my eyes never leaving sight of the bobbing heads on the road.

'Look at them, Gary.' I point. 'These poor people are viewed with distaste by the government. They have been internally displaced for political gain when all they wanted was to keep their jobs.'

We stare at each other. This is really happening. For the last eighteen months the labourers on our farm have been targeted by the local war vets and many of them have been subjected to violence in different forms, and now they have to leave with a gratuity in their pockets and not much more. They are all being chased by the punishing hot breath of the homeless winds. The domestics will be moving with us. They have collected various pieces of furniture over the years and their belongings will be loaded on the lorry with ours.

All tractors, save one, which has been commandeered by the harridan and her motley crew have been taken off the farm. This operation has been done over the past weeks at varying times of the day and shipped to the flower farm. Equipment and irrigation pipes have slowly disappeared into thin air; not an easy task with so many eyes watching our every move.

Packing crates and boxes clutter up the house for the following week. Photograph Frames, pictures and other wall hangings pile up on the dining room table leaving the walls empty; a sad echo of their former selves. I find myself walking aimlessly from room to room opening and closing cupboard doors. I have already transported all the pot plants to the new house and the veranda looks barren. Water marks stain the veranda floor leaving me in no doubt as to how many pots had been responsible for the tropical haven we had created. I idly ponder on whether I should sweep the house and then pull myself up thinking 'that is the most ridiculous thing I've ever heard,' before snorting; had I spoken out aloud? The week gallops by with alarming speed and with the day for moving suddenly more or less on top of us, my bravado is slipping, leaving a queasy pressure building beneath my midriff.

Chapter 28

BROKEN WINDOWS

The Sunday before we leave the farm, we are invited to a young couple Stu (who had been one of the men abducted and beaten when Dave Stevens had been murdered) and Lise for lunch. There are twelve of us and we sit soaking up the sun and wine over a delicious meal. I sink into my deck chair listening to the laughter. Stretching my legs out straight I can feel the pull on my muscles before relaxing them, and concentrating on letting my shoulders drop. The long months of living with stress had taken its toll on my neck and shoulders, which are taut. I sip on my wine savouring and enjoying the full bodied taste; swirling it around my mouth before gently swallowing. The smell of the chicken cooking on the braai teases my taste buds and I look longingly at the table which is laden with salads, garlic bread, pickles and other delicious looking treats.

'Bloody price of black market fuel is a nightmare. These bastards are just exploiting us. Everyone is jumping on the bandwagon.' The conversation inevitably turns back to the reality of today.

'Oh, no you don't. No talk of politics, war vets or any other shit today,' Stu refills the wine glasses before disappearing to restock on cold beers. 'Anyone mentions any of the above will have to down a glass of alcohol, okay?' He slurs slightly on his return.

'We can meet up for a game of golf in Marondera.' Ant suggests and I have a chuckle. It is a long time since the two of us walked the golf course bashing at a stationary ball. 'You never know, our game might have improved.' She stares over at Al, her husband who is tall and good looking with a ready laugh. 'We can even spend a night here and there, especially after Al has been to golf.'

'Oh, Ant that would be fantastic because we feel a bit nervous leaving the district. I can't describe how I feel inside. It's like numbness has taken over – an unreality and I keep expecting to wake up sweating from the nightmare.'

'Is Gary going to enjoy his job?' She asks. 'It's going to be hard when you've been your own boss.'

'You know, we are so grateful to have a job. It is well paid, and money and stability is what we need. For the last ten days, we have been watching the labour leave the farm. It is heart breaking. I hate it. I just don't know where this is all going to end.' I quaver, looking away, but she has noticed the tears threatening, and pops her hand on my forearm, rubbing gently. 'I just need to get through tomorrow. Oh, Ant how we have all moved the boundaries. We all seem to have to give more and more to these people; I don't want to go, but I do want to leave.'

Her two little boys dance up, chewing on pieces of chicken, and sporting huge smiles. Ant and Al both grew up in the district, and went on to marry. They are an integral part of Virginia life, and a popular young couple, with their good looks and gorgeous kids. We move on to chatting about school and sport.

A breeze has dispersed the clouds which billowed up over lunch, allowing the afternoon sunshine to creep into our circle warming our feet and causing elongated shadows; an illusion of perfect bliss. I close my eyes briefly and listen to the tinkle of laughter interspersed with the low coo-doo-doo chuckling call of the laughing doves. I feel relaxed and a little heady after the wine and loath to leave. The thoughts inside my head are on a roller coaster ride. I know that yesterday is dead and we have to now look to the future. The lunch has passed in a hazy whirl, and now it is back to reality.

Gary catches my eye and we both reluctantly push ourselves slowly to our feet. With words catching at the back of my throat and tears clinging to my eyelashes, I climb into the passenger seat of the car. I watch the small group of people waving until they are swallowed up in the dust. We are leaving the following day, and it is essential that we seal packing crates tonight as the lorry will be with us first thing in the morning. We are one of the first couples to leave the district and it is a harsh reality to the others of their own fate.

This will be the last time that we will be driving this road, in the district that we have called home over the last twenty years. The house is in a turmoil; crates and boxes everywhere. Furniture has been pushed together, glared upon by empty walls and undressed windows. It takes us a couple of hours to tie up the loose ends. Gary finds me perched on a packing crate, a wingless bird staring off into the distance. I have already said my goodbyes to our home and garden but here I am sitting, feeling surreal and numb. The fiery sunset is slipping behind the trees; a swansong to our last evening on the farm. I feel that my control is slipping through my fingers as I watch the last light caress my garden goodnight and goodbye.

We pour ourselves a drink, clinking glasses gently; not celebrating but acknowledging the fact that it is an end of a happy era for both of us. The dogs lie curled up on their mats at my feet enjoying the attention from my toes.

'I think we are pretty much done and dusted now, Gary.' I stand lighting a cigarette and open one of the beautiful earthy oregon pine french doors leading out onto the empty veranda. 'I have been so happy here on this farm. Thank you.' I look at him, and then at the doors. 'I hate that we have to leave these behind. I drag on the cigarette, inhaling and watching the tendrils of smoke drift lazily in the slight breeze; long smoky grey vapour trails. 'It is strange how we worry about things like Oregon pine doors when we are losing our farm. How weird is that?' I am mumbling more to myself, not expecting Gary to answer me. I turn to look at him and smile sadly. He is looking like I am feeling; a shadow of our former cheerful selves.

'I never believed that this day would come.' I whisper.

'Jen, who knows where our destiny will take us; but we are, physically in one piece. Our first concern is the folks, and making sure that they are going to be okay.' I smile at him without voicing my thoughts. 'The horses are up on the next door farm, so we don't have to face having them destroyed just yet.' Our Brahman cross cow had been shot, a thought that I find hard to swallow after all her escapes from the cold storage lorry.

'All this destruction, it just makes my hair curl. Maggie died too young, Gary. I know the nurse at the clinic said she probably had a heart attack, and that seems plausible, but you wonder if it was not just the stress caused from these people. She will forever be in my heart. I always knew from the moment I met her that our footprints would be left side by side along the same road. I just never imagined I would have to leave her behind; or maybe she has left me behind? I miss her. Would you like another drink?' He nods at me.

I am standing on the first step leading out of the lounge when I hear Ant screaming. It bursts out over our security radio sounding distorted and loud as it bounces off the walls. It is blood chilling, the hair on the nape of my neck prickles and I drop the glass. It shatters onto the floor with a loud splintering crash, sending small shards of glass skidding over the tiles. The dogs react instantly; growling, barking and incensed by the desperate and primeval screams echoing

192

around the empty room. Gary is airborne out of his chair clasping a hand to his mouth, knocking the small side table over with a loud bang. Forgetting the shattered glass we stand silently, listening to Ant's hysterical calls for help. The two little boys are screaming loudly in the background. What the hell is going on? They had been at the lunch today with us and here she is screaming that Al is dead.

'He has been shot.' She is screaming. 'A war vet ambushed us by putting branches across the road.'

Before Al can open the door to get out enabling him to heave the branches aside, one of their resident war veterans shot him. The ambush had given the war veteran time to appear out of the bush, raise the rifle and taking aim he pulled the trigger. He shot Al, who is sitting in the passenger seat with their little boy on his lap through the driver's window shattering the glass and fragmenting the bullet. Ant manages to drive away from the scene, all the while begging for someone to please come and help her. Andrew, a fellow farmer, who lives close to the Bradleys answers her distress call and promises to meet her at their turnoff.

'I think Al is dead - oh my god, he is covered in blood.' Her screams make the hair on the nape of my neck stand up. 'There is blood all over the front of the car.'

'Ant, just keep driving. I am on my way and will meet you at the turnoff.' Andrews' calm tone soothes the airwaves. 'I will be there, just keep going.'

'Andrew, I can't wake him. He can't hear me.' She sobs. 'He can't hear me. He is slumped in the seat. Oh god, Al, wake up please.'

Ant drives her family off the farm; keeping her head while she negotiates the bumps and corners of the farm road at a high speed. Andrew is waiting for her at the main road. He had already alerted

Borrowdaille Hospital, Marondera of the emergency. Andrew feels for a pulse, assuring her that he is still alive, but Al needs assistance and fast. Ant's mum and dad are also waiting on the road for Ant. Once we know that someone is there to assist Ant and Al, I turn with a look of horror on my face, to Gary. His face is still, a mask so deathly pale that I tap him on the shoulder, watching an expression of disbelief flicker in his eyes. He lights us both a cigarette, handing me one with trembling fingers.

My chest feels tight and I stub out the cigarette, recoiling slightly at the stale smell of the ashtray. We do not know how bad Al is, but what we had heard over the radio has been the sound of a young family going through hell. I will never forget the echoes of those little boys screaming and Ant's distressed calls for help.

'Oh, Gary, I don't know why anyone would want to shoot Al?' I shake my head, losing control and sobbing onto his shoulder. He holds me, and our tears mingle; united in our grief of all things violent. The dogs lie as close as they can to my chair, while we sit waiting late into the night, for an update on Alan's condition. He has been transferred from Borrowdaille through to the Avenues Clinic in Harare.

Daybreak eventually creeps through the bedroom window and a slow cloud of dust follows the lorry as it crawls down the road. The domestics help to load the lorry. It is a desolate scene depicting the tragedy unfolding over Zimbabwe. Adam's eyes are downcast, his mouth as tight as a gash across his face as he takes a last walk through the empty house with me. Our footsteps echo loudly as we check each room. In the bathroom I retrieve my toothbrush and the toothpaste which has been used more than once this morning. I had spent a restless night trying to close my mind to the evening's tragedy. No amount of teeth brushing seems to help; my mouth feels dry and disgusting; a result of too many cigarettes and coffee throughout the long slow hours of darkness.

I wander around my garden, stopping off at the bird aviary. I am so relieved that Rod (a friend) is going to pick up all our birds within the hour. I kneel down chatting to the guinea fowl through the wire mesh feeling hot tears prickling my eyelids, overflowing and sliding in warm trickles down my cheeks. The bird mesh is too small and I can only push one finger through trying to make contact with the guinea fowl; panic is seeping through and crushing my chest. I desperately try to make last minute images, but my memories keep tangling and spiralling away into darkness. Gary bends over taking my elbow gently. He helps me to my feet.

'Come on Hon. Let's get going.' I walk back towards the house, gathering my thoughts and wrapping them around me like a blanket. I need to be strong.

'I don't want to leave.' My voice is full of panic. I burst into tears and the two of us stand, holding each other close. 'I am not going to wait for Rod. I have to go now, or else I am going to make a total idiot of myself.' I brush away the tears. I am sitting in the car and revving the engine when I hear a little tap on the window. It is Rod. I have been unaware of his arrival. I climb out, giving him a hug. It does not take him long to catch the remaining birds, and I watch through blurred eyes as he loads them into the back of his closed truck. He gives me another hug.

'I will look after them all.' He promises. 'The birds I collected on Friday are all looking good, Jen.' I don't bring up the subject of Al, because I have been listening to him and Gary discussing the tragedy.

The dogs have been shadowing my left heel and leap into the back seat of the car as soon as I open the door. I edge the vehicle towards the security fence gate. I am going to wait for Gary at the top of the road. I have to drive past the harridan and the other war vets who have gathered to watch us leave. They are like bloody vultures, waiting to swoop in on my beautiful home. I slow down as I know Gary is going to have a problem leaving. They are threatening to not let Gary leave the fence, until he hands over the house keys. I trundle up the road slowly, trying to memorise all the surroundings that I am so passionate about. I stop at the top of the hill, and climb out of the vehicle. I gaze down over the valley that was our home. The trees, if they survive will be witness to the rampant destruction that is going to take place on our farm. We are leaving the district after twenty years and my bleeding heart is cavorting around my chest. The scene before me looks so peaceful; and yet it is hiding a secret of violence and theft.

I breathe out, relieved to see Gary's truck coming around the corner. Clambering back in, I drive to our turn off at the main road. Loathe at abandoning our past just yet, I find my foot pressing down on the brake. Our sign post has been kicked over. Indents from angry boots have bent and buckled it. I stare at it through eyes that are misted, and yet I feel that there are no more tears left to cry. It has been treated with the same disrespect that we have been shown over the last eighteen months. Next to our bent sign is a new one, scrawled in spidery writing with red paint that reads 'KEEP OFF, WAR VETERANS. NO GO AREA.'

I do not remember the countryside roaring by; brushstrokes of emptiness. I lead the way to the new house.

Our furniture is all in place by that evening. We have had an update on Al's condition. He is in an induced coma and still nowhere near being out of the woods. I bump into Ant a few days after we have moved, and she looks so little and tired; her face is covered in small angry nicks from the broken glass. I put my arms around her, hugging her tight, praying that Al will survive.

After hearing her story which is repeated in a monotone voice, my head whispers that we have done the right thing by leaving. I just cannot credit how any adult could not only aim a weapon, but actually pull the trigger on another human being, let alone one who actually had a small child sitting on their lap. Leaving Ant and driving back to our new home, my eye keeps being drawn to the star crack in the windscreen. My ears keep hearing my glass breaking on the floor the night we heard Ant screaming, and her driver's window shattering as the bullets hit it. 'Broken windows' seems to sum up our move off the farm.

A war veteran is arrested for shooting Al, and his reason behind the violence was; he thought he had better shoot Al before Al shot him. He is released with no charge.

Chapter 29

AFTER THE STORM

We had been living away from the farm for a couple of weeks already; time well used to soothe our souls and lick our wounds. Living so close to town has opened up a whole new world for us. We can see the lights from Malwatte Restaurant twinkling like stars at night; offering a comforting thought of civilisation within a stone's throw away. Most evenings we fight it out on the tennis court, laughing at how rusty our game has become, but enjoying the exercise anyway. The indoor swimming pool is enclosed in the covered court yard and having tested the temperature of the water with my big toe and shivering with cold, we seldom swim. The house sits foursquare and ugly but once inside, the rooms are spacious and easy to decorate. With the house being situated right on the main road, we are inundated with visitors. We can also buy take-a-ways from the Malwatte Restaurant.

'Imagine getting excited about being able to have a take -a - way Gary' I laugh at our excitement, 'How lucky are we?'

Ben is writing his first year 'A' levels. He is still a border, but with our move we are now only fifteen minutes from the school. Ben with a grin puts a claim on the green Mazda twin cab.

'I will take the Mazda off your hands Dad. It will give you more room for parking' he smiles, gently putting the pressure on. I chuckle as he runs his hand lovingly over the bonnet, before looking around the spacious drive way. 'If you need her, then shout and I will have her back to you in a tick.'

'Oh, Ben, I love your sense of confidence. Anyway, you are right. I don't need the vehicle, and,' he sweeps an arm around the spacious driveway, 'we do need extra parking!'

'Oh, Dad, you're genius, thank you so much. I promise I will look after her.' He runs his hand along the side of car, caressing her lovingly. 'She is a real beaut.' His grin is wide, and I catch a glimpse of white teeth.

Gary has the use of a company vehicle and I have my car. So, Ben becomes independent. He has the freedom during term time to come and go as he pleases. I am delighted as I see him a couple of times a week. He is continually hungry. Some days I get home from town and the kitchen counter looks like a loaf of bread has exploded; crumbs and droplets of marmalade everywhere. The whir of the washing machine tells me that Ben has also arrived with his large laundry bag full of dirty washing.

Edna's smooth dark skin is healthy and youthful. Her dark eyes' have lost their haunted look. She misses her mum, but, I have noticed little quips of humour again. She is a totally different character to her mum, padding quietly around the house seeing to her chores. I miss the banter with Maggie. Mikaela is in Harare and we see as much of her as we can.

A couple of weeks into our move, I get a phone call asking me if I would be interested in taking up a teaching post at the Girls School a couple of kilometres down the road. I immediately decline the offer before berating myself.

'Oh damn, Gary, I am such a coward.' We sit down to eat our supper.

'It's not too late to change your mind. Just give her a ring back.' he retorts, picking up the pepper grinder and speckling his food with coarse black pepper. We change the subject to his new job. He is learning the art of growing hectares and hectares of hypericum berries for export into Holland.

'I am really enjoying it, Jen, but it is going to frustrate me until we can get the soil ph. balance right. However, you know what I am like and once I get to grips with this new venture, I will be happy. It is going to be good money for us, and for now I just need to produce the goods and hope that we survive a few seasons without interruptions from the war vets.' He rubs his hands together and I burst out laughing. He looks charmingly avaricious.

The following morning I am still dithering on whether I should phone Harriet back when she phones me. 'Come on, Jen, we really need you. You will do a great job having done your art course. You will honestly just need to show the girls the very basics of art. You can do it.' She was very persuasive and makes it all sound so easy.

'Okay Harriet, I will do it. Maybe we can meet up later and then I will have an idea of exactly what will be expected of me'. I agree with my heart hammering. After I put the phone down, I feel a pleasant tingle in my heart. I have committed myself and immediately my mind starts planning ahead, preparing me for the following term.

By the beginning of the next term I set off for school feeling excited and nervous. I have no idea what to expect. My first class will comprise of twenty eight girls.

'I have twenty eight girls in my class and all of them will probably be hormonal.' I wince, whispering into the phone to Gary. 'I don't know if I can do this.'

'You are worried about facing twenty eight young girls, Jen.' He bursts out laughing. 'What on earth are you worried about? Having been through some of the incidents on the farm, and here you are worrying about a bunch of girls. You must be joking?' His laughter has made me chuckle.

'Ja, I am worried about them, but you are right. I love you and will phone you after my first lesson; if I survive.' I ring off. When the bell rings, I can feel the butterflies fluttering madly around my stomach prompting me to take slow breaths before I pop my head out the art room door. All the girls are lined up outside the classroom and I can feel twenty eight pairs of eyes looking me up and down. I invite them all in, and after introducing myself; I get down to teaching the first lesson, praying that I will not make a total fool of myself. We all get through the first double lesson and after they have left the room, I realise how much I have loved the past hour. I had been unsure of myself, but had overcome it and the girls showed signs of enjoying themselves; which is something I want to teach them; a love of art. As the term wears on I relax, and always look forward to the time spent with my class.

The school is like an oasis for me, soothing but busy. There is no talk of politics, war veterans or displaced farmers. As I enter the gates, parking my car under the large Msasa tree, the cares and worries vacate leaving a warm fuzzy happiness in the pit of my tummy. I begin to live for the moment. The art room is a safe haven for the girls. The walls are covered with a variety of artwork, a colourful patchwork of different techniques, brush strokes and talent. The wonderful smell of paint lingers, ingrained in the desks that have seen many students passing through over the years. The infusion of colour and scent adds to the inviting atmosphere that pervades the art room, artistically beckoning and embracing the variety of students who use it. It is a gloriously messy and busy room. I am teaching a cross section of girls from all different walks of life, and each and every one of them adds their personal touch to my week. The morning is all about art lessons and the afternoon is spent being creative with arts and crafts. I love it.

Leaving the school gates at the end of an afternoon is like arriving back into a reality check. We keep abreast of all that is happening in the country and nothing has changed. Our district is still experiencing problems on a daily basis and more farmers are being removed from their homes, and having to leave the area. I spend long hours, like all of us mere mortals parked patiently in long queues that can snake for over a kilometre to get fuel. But these queues have become a great meeting place where one can hear the laughter of good humoured Zimbabweans. We are all making 'a plan' to overcome all the disabilities of living daily in our beloved country. Power cuts and fuel shortages don't seem so bad when you sit on your folding chair slurping a beer and chatting to friends. I am living a double life; one of normality behind school gates, and my re-entry into chaos at the end of my shifts.

Zimbabwe has one of the highest rates of HIV infection in the world, food shortages, and an inflation that is out of control; over half of the population is living in poverty.

Towards the end of the year our friends Paul and Mags have had their marching orders. They are being forced from their farm in the district. They have found a house in Marondera and are looking forward to getting some control back into their lives. Paul and Gary are now facing a huge problem; horses. Paul had kindly allowed our two remaining horses to run with theirs.

'Jen, Paul and I have been talking and I think that we are going to phone the man who runs the croc farm.' He tentatively broaches the subject.

'What!!' I spit. 'You have got to be joking.' My eyes are flashing. 'You are going to allow our remaining horses to be eaten by crocs.' I am stamping my foot, tears overflowing and running down my cheeks. 'How can you just say you are going to feed them to the crocs? What the hell is wrong with you?' I slam the door, slumping onto my bed, trying to get away from the awful images that are flashing through my mind. 'We could not bear the thought of Mercy Me going to the croc farm and saved her. Now, we are going to send her there ourselves.' I am ranting at him through the closed door.

'Jen, stop it.' Gary's voice is firm as he opens the door. I look up at him; his eyebrows frowning and angry. 'We are going to have to shoot the horses, and then they will be fed to the crocs.' He is angry, a whiteness creasing around his eyes. 'What the hell do you think I am going to do? Throw them to the crocs?' He turns around, slamming the door behind him. 'Grow up, you silly woman. You are being a total pain in the arse.' He shouts through the door, and I sit up with a dumbfounded expression on my face.

'How dare you yell at me to grow up, or tell me I am a pain in the arse!' I retort. I turn my face to the wall, my heart beating rapidly. 'Gary...why has it all come to this.' I mutter, burying my damp cheeks in the pillow.

I rinse cold water over my face, staring at my pale reflection in the mirror. I wander down the passage and up to the lounge. Gary is leaning forward on the couch and I can see from the stillness that he is desperately sad. My heart turns over. 'I am sorry, Gary.' I touch his elbow and he turns with such a defeated look in his eye. I wrap my arms around his neck. 'I am sorry. I just went crazy there.'

'I don't want to destroy those magnificent beasts anymore than you do.' His voice catches, 'but,' he hesitates, 'I don't know what else we can do, Jen.' He stares off. 'Nobody wants them. There has been too much destruction already. It tears me apart.'

'Gary, will they blindfold the horses?' I whisper.

'Yes.' I hug him and turn before he can see the despair in my eyes. I can feel my stomach heaving. Horses have become sad victims along with the rest of us. A heavy cloud, weighed down with guilt burdens my every shadow; a cloud that I will have to confront and shed before it imprisons me.

'It is the guilt of knowing what we have to do, Gary. We have had to destroy everything we love, and now we are left with Toffee and Beano. The guilt of having to leave the wild life that we were privileged enough to share the farm with. All those people who worked for us.... what is going to happen to them?' I plod inside, dragging the shadow with me. I will have to open this bag of guilt that I am dragging behind me, but only when I feel strong enough.

I am in town on the day that our horses, along with Pauls' are loaded onto the lorry and shot. Gary phones me to let me know that it had all been done. Even though I have been waiting for the call, emotion that has been locked firmly in the shadows of my mind reaches out, grabbing my heart. I hit the brakes and pull into a parking, putting my head down on the steering wheel, sobbing; tears of sadness, frustration and anger. A light tap on the car window disturbs me. I look up though a mist of tears at a little grey haired lady with milky eyes staring at me, worry all over her face. 'Are you okay, dear?' I open the window.

'I...'m fine.' She puts her wrinkled hand onto my arm, squeezing gently and cocking her head.

'Come on, you can tell me.' Her fingers close gently over my wrist, concern in her voice.

'We have just had two of our remaining horses put down, and it's tearing me apart.' My voice is croaky with emotion. 'I will be okay. I just feel raw.' I sniff. 'And horribly guilty.' I add, blowing my nose.

'Are you a farmer's wife?' I nod the affirmative. 'I am so sorry to hear about your horses, dear. Our country is not a good place anymore. Would you like a cup of coffee? We can talk.' I climb out of the car, reaching for her well manicured hand.

'Thank you so much for stopping. I will be fine. Our country is in a mess, but what amazing people live here.' I look at this dear little lady. 'I am on my way to my sisters for lunch, and she breaks from 1.00 until two.' I look down at my watch and I have about eight minutes. She leans over, giving me a hug. This total stranger cares. That is a heart warming thought. 'Thank you.'

'Good luck dear. I hope everything turns out well for you.' She smiles, a sad look clouding her milky eyes. I realise how lucky we are. We are still young enough to make a life. I watch as she trots off down the pavement, little silver bun winking at the sun. She turns and I wave.

Many of our friends and associates are at this stage leaving the country; looking for a better and safer life elsewhere. Al has recovered from his shooting incident and they are making plans to relocate to New Zealand. These two friends are making life changing decision and I feel uncomfortable with this fact.

My first year of teaching is coming to an end and I have loved every minute of it. During the afternoons the art room is full of girls; bundles of hormonal energy producing paintings that explode with colour and imagination. Sunlight streams through the open windows, poking into dark corners. Through the windows small insects buzz with fervour, minute gossamer wings shimmering as they caress the flower beds bursting with blossoms. Pollen floats through the window, miniscule particles of pixie dust. Our art room is an oasis compared to the troubled world that resides beyond the school gates.

The devaluation of our Zimbabwean dollar is rocketing out of control and so, we are as a country, experiencing a shortage of cash; sounds crazy but true. Times are tough. With another election looming, we keep our heads down and hope that we will all get through it. More farmers lose their livelihoods and there are endless MDC activists murdered. Through the political turmoil and violence that has become a part of the lives of all Zimbabweans, we continue to try and make a life for ourselves.

Gary's Zimbabwe passport has expired and the authorities will not renew it. I stomp my feet at the injustice of him being told that he does not qualify for a passport. Gary's dad was born in South Africa and the authorities want Gary to renounce the right to his fathers' birth right. The whole argument is ludicrous and when he refuses to renounce his fathers' birth right, the embassy refuses to allow him a Zimbabwean passport.

'That is fine, Jen. I will apply for a South African one.' He is angry as for the past thirty odd years of him having a Zimbabwe passport, this issue has never come up before.

Mugabe wins the Presidential elections and a comment from the opposition leader, 'the election results do not reflect the true will of the people and are consequently illegitimate' has me nodding my head in agreement. He then adds, 'we seek no confrontation with the state, because that is what it is looking for. We foresaw electoral fraud but not daylight robbery.' I burst out laughing and Gary, who happens to be walking past the door, pops his head in.

'That laughter sounds good. What are you laughing at?' and when I explain, we both give the picture of Mugabe on TV the finger, then I pull a tongue at his image, tasting past youth. It is childish. Yes. But it makes me feel better.

The mutilated body of a farmer, Terry Ford is found on the morning of the 18th March 2002. His little jack russell, Squeak, who has been his companion for 14 years, is keeping watch over his body with anxious eyes. The pounding of his small heart is the only sound to be heard in the quiet darkness. Violence lingers in the air, dimming the stars once the footsteps of the perpetrators has faded, like cowards into the shadows. The police, who have long abandoned the road of justice, had refused to come to his aid. The report hints at signs of torture and the very same police, who had refused to come to his aid, come for the body.

Gary, Lorraine (my teaching friend) and I drive through to the Presbyterian Church in Harare for the funeral.

'Look at that little dog, Gary.' I whisper, tears spilling over as I nod towards Squeak, as he is being led into the church, his little grey muzzle and dark nose twitching. 'He is a silent witness to a terrible crime.' I blow my nose. This little dog has been splashed on the front page of many news papers worldwide. 'It is hard to not allow our feelings to become poisoned. When the hell is this going to end, or is it?' Lorraine takes my arm and the three of us enter the church with heavy hearts. I sit quietly, searching for answers and imagining Terry Ford's spirit alone with the wind. His family and friends will unite in their grief. A heavy silence of loss lingers long after the service is finished.

The following afternoon, a couple of the girls find me in the art room. They are being chased by ghostly shadows of our increasingly violent world. They have heard about the latest murder, and the burden of worry sits heavily on their shoulders. Their parents are farming. We sit the three of us, and I find my eyes brimming with tears as I see the fear reflected in theirs. What can I tell them?

Our year's lease is up and the owners have put the house on the market. We again pack up our belongings and move into a large sprawling house in Marondera. Adam and Edna come with us.

Chapter 30

SAND, SUN AND PINKIE PROMISES

After a few evenings spent around the dinner table with a group of friends discussing a holiday, we decide that sinking our bodies into the warm salty sea is the ideal setting to escape to; to come terms with the strong currents of change sweeping through the country.

After packing up the various trucks and the huge sea going fishing boat, we start the nine hour trip. The last half hour of the journey is spent weaving along the small coastal dirt road, where the thick beach sand constantly threatens to swallow the wheels. The heady smell of the ocean seduces the late afternoon pulling the long shadows through the fine salty mist that settles on our warm skin.

Arriving at the two houses sitting squat and fore square, we scurry around like ants unpacking the vehicles and the large boat. Eelco, Andre (farming friends) and Gary reverse the big boat into the gentle waves, floating it off the trailer and into the warm arms of the sea. What had looked so enormous on the trailer now looks no bigger than a toy on a pond.

'And, now we are ready for a sun downer.' Gary's brown face is creased with smiles, his green fishing cap with its worm smudged peak firmly pulled down over his forehead, 'Jen, the boat is big enough.' He ruffles my hair, laughing at my earlier question. Life is warm.

'Life cannot get more perfect than this.' I turn to Lo, an old school friend whom I love dearly and Laura (Andre's wife) as we watch the African sun bowing gently below the horizon on the orange sea. 'Gin and tonics, here we come.' We raise our glasses, listening as the gentle soothing lapping of the waves bestows salty kisses on the toasted sand.

Within days, our bodies are as brown as berries. We spend endless hours walking barefoot along the beach and wiggling our toes in the tepid Indian Ocean. Under the warm watch of the African sun, we shed our tensions along with our clothes as we enjoy the balminess on our bare shoulders. The wide rustic veranda offers shade from the midday sun and all our meals are eaten sitting around the long dining table, a noisy jolly affair with much laughter and leg pulling. Fresh fish is prepared and fillets are barbequed. The chef of the day has to keep sneaking fingers under control, as we all stand close like scavengers, our mouths watering, as the divine smoky smells tickle our taste buds.

'You men are slacking. We need more supplies of fish.' Lois smacks her lips with pleasure. 'Useless bloody fishermen we have in our camp, girls.' The men laugh their reply.

We spend the days riding the waves, squealing with delight as the boat ploughs through the swells covering us with a fine salty spray.

'Look over there.' I am pointing, my voice quivering with excitement. 'Dolphins, Eelco.'

'Slow down, Eelco.' We all shout in unison, clapping as the front of the boat drops back gently, the warm ocean licking our toes as he slows down, steering towards them. Putting the boat back up on the plane, the ocean erupts with life and they are swimming between the pods of the boat. Their sleek graceful bodies cut through the water with powerful precision and turning to keep an eye on us they appear to grin at our applause. If my legs were longer, I could point my toes and feel the silky bodies skimming through the water below me. The magic of the moment feeds my spirit as the warmth of the continent pulses through my veins and the realization hits me; I am a blue eyed person with an African soul. I turn to look at the others on the boat and they all have a look of childish delight, huge grins creasing brown healthy faces and eyes as bright as the morning sun.

'That was amazing, Eelco. Maybe they will be here at the same time tomorrow.' I shout over the wind, giving him the thumbs up sign. I laugh out loud sharing my enjoyment; the wind races through my hair, whipping my face and neck and I sit at the front of the boat, holding tight enjoying the salty taste on my lips. The feeling of gliding through the air is intoxicating; flying without wings. The ocean colours reflect the mood on the boat as we ride the waves on this magnificent cerulean playground.

Paradise Island is a mere 2.3km in length, surrounded by turquoise waters and milky beaches. The shallow reef provides us with hours of snorkelling. Vivid colours and crackling coral have me yearning for more visual feasts. I am lost in this underwater paradise, forgetting I have legs, opting to become one with the aquatic life. This vibrant world is peaceful, lulled to and fro by the gentle current as a school of parrot fish part and close around me, and I drift amongst the cosmic colours, never wanting to leave. This has to be heaven.

The men are enjoying endless hours of deep sea fishing; some days arriving back at camp with a keep net full of 'dinner'. The evenings are spent listening to the rhythmic pounding of the waves as they wash away a myriad of footprints leaving the beach clean and untouched for the duration of the night.

Climbing out from under the protective folds of the mosquito net, I stretch lazily, arching my back before slipping my feet into my flip flops and making my way to the bathroom. The sun rises over the ocean, a golden sphere of energy spreading warmth over the gently undulating water as she reaches up kissing the sky. I stand, refreshed from a good night's sleep sipping on hot sweet condensed milk coffee as I watch the fisherman paddle out to sea. The early sunlight bathes the dhows, trickling a gilt edged halo of reflections as the oars move rhythmically pushing the dhow out and over the swells. The early morning breeze carries melancholy echoes from the depths of the ocean, songs of praise from another world. Closing my eyes, I wallow in the warmth of the harmony, my limbs like liquid as the mellow sun cradles my sun browned body in a toasty caress.

'What a life, Jen.' I turn as Gary pops his arm around my shoulders. 'Maybe we could all look at running a holiday camp.' He grins, waving an arm, enveloping the ocean. 'This could be our front garden.' His mind is always whirring, constantly turning over thinking of where our road is going to take us.

'Look.' I point at the sky, 'not a cloud in sight. Let's not waste a minute more and go enjoy another perfect day with all of us amazing people in paradise.' I smile. We tear our gaze away from the ocean, turning to refill our mugs with roasted sweet coffee, blowing gently as the steam rises. The aroma drifts through the open windows enticing our friends to leave the warmth of their beds. This has been the most perfect three weeks of sand, sun shine and gin and tonics. There has been no talk of farm invasions or war vets. All too soon it is time to pack up camp. We feel relaxed, happy and ready to face the months ahead.

Once through the border posts, we trundle slowly up the Christmas Pass before hooting and waving goodbye to our friends as we overtake them. Just past the Drifters back pack resort, Gary indicates right and we turn onto the dirt road, manoeuvring carefully around the pot holes as we make our way slowly up to the security fence, arriving in a thick swirl of dust. Gary grins. 'I am looking forward to spending the night and catching up with Biff and Ken Styles.'

'I am too.' I hang my handbag over a shoulder, grabbing the bottle of vodka that has been tucked up safely between us on the front seat. 'Party time' I wrinkle my nose at Gary. It is what we call my mischievous look. Biff appears from around the corner, warm smile lighting up her face.

'Vodka...' The smile grows. 'I feel a party coming on.' I am enveloped in a big bear hug.

Knight (Biff's cook) claps both hands together, greeting us in his singsong voice 'Kanjani, Medemmm.' He exaggerates his words, dragging them out, his grey moustache waggling merrily above a gummy grin.

'Kanjani Knight.' We greet him back, shaking his bony hand. This wizened old gentleman, his tight grey curls hugging his head has worked for Biff and Ken for 25 years. He runs the household, his starched khaki trousers ironed to perfection and a new pair of glasses enables his tired old eyes to see clearly.

'That was absolutely delicious, Biff. I don't know how he does it.' I compliment the cook. The roast beef had been cooked to perfection, underdone and juicy. Fresh green peas, runner beans, crisp golden brown roast potatoes and mashed butternut smoothed out with a lump of butter. I use my finger to mop up a small spot of delicious meaty gravy. With stomachs full to popping we all sit chatting; both Gary and I regaling them with fishing and snorkelling stories, turning Ken green with envy at the pictures of all the huge fish. Unfortunately there are also more tales of desperate farmers and their labour having to evacuate their farms under the most horrendous circumstances. I sigh inside; we should have stayed put on the beach with the freedom of the space and the water. Reality is hard to face, and nothing has changed while we have been away.

The clock chimes 12.30 and the two men, full to busting with good food and beer weave their weave their way upstairs to hit the sack.

Biff and I have been friends since she was fourteen and I was fifteen. I love her like a sister and our lives have touched and parted for many years. Our lively chatter does not stop amid much glass clinking, laughter and tears. By two o'clock in the morning our conversation is to put it bluntly a load of bull shit. Biffs' taps trickle tears down her rosy cheeks, and I hand her a tissue and she wipes her eyes with a grin.

'You have not changed one little bit over the years, Biff. You still cry at the drop of hat.' I am laughing. 'I would hate to see you really upset, it would be like a flood.'

We trash over all the escapades we had got up to in our teenage years and I am wetting myself at her drunken descriptions of our roof rattling evenings. Her short brown hair is as boisterous as she is and her cheeks are rosy as she embraces life to the full, eyes twinkling wickedly.

'What are you and Gary going to do? I know he is enjoying growing the flowers, but I worry about you both. Another one of my friends has left, Jen. They have gone back to Holland.' Her rabbit mind changes direction, yet again. Biff is well aware of the toll that the last eighteen months of living with the war vets has had on us both. They are having the same problems.

'Biff I don't know what we are going to do. Gary has been making enquiries, but hey, we have my folks to think about, and I can't see us leaving them behind.' I laugh. 'At this stage Gary is trying to put aside as much money as he can. Australia is beckoning but we need more years here before we can move on. We are not going anywhere fast, of that I can promise you'.

'Well good, Jen. We will be putting out the lights together then.' A standard joke on who will be last to leave the country.

She leans over grabbing my hand while we sit grinning at each other like two kids, our little fingers entwined before Biff splutters, 'pinkie promise, Jen. I want you to make a pinkie promise that you are not going to up and leave Zimbabwe.'

'I make you a pinkie promise that we will not up and leave Zimbabwe. Lets seal my pinkie promise with another drink okay'. Our serious pact is cast in little fingers and vodka. The following morning I climb out of my bed with a grim headache and grin ruefully at Gary. 'Yikes, Biff and I got through a lot of old stories last night.'

'I would say you washed those stories down with a lot of vodka too,' Gary smiles at me.

'Oh yes we did,' I laugh out loud and cringe, putting my hands up to hold my thumping head, which has geared up a notch.

'Oh please, Gary, some disprins would be good.'

Biff is also looking about as fresh as yesterday's breakfast. Our jolly behaviour from the night before is over. We push down a cooked breakfast before saying our goodbyes and the two of us hold up our little pinkies. 'Pinkie promise, Biff.' I wave out the window and then we are on the road again, leaving in a cloud of dust. Over the next year we talk often over the phone, and giggle about the 'pinkie promise' before discussing how many people are now leaving the country.

Chapter 31

FLYING DOWN UNDER

March 19th 2003 is the start of what becomes known as the 'Iraq War' or 'Operation Iraqi'; combined forces from the United States and the United Kingdom and smaller contingents from Australia and Poland invade Iraq to topple Saddam Hussein's regime. I have been getting through the days since one of my old and dear friend Barbs has flown the coop, immigrating to the UK. It has been hard and I miss her. Our trip has come just at the right time. We have our tickets booked to fly to Australia and we will be boarding the plane on the 1st April, 2003. This will be our first visit to a first world country and we are buzzing with excitement. We cross the border post between Zimbabwe and South Africa at Beitbridge boarder post minus the 'operation chicken sandwich.'

'What is your destination?' The overweight official asks with a pleasant smile.

'We are heading for Johannesburg airport where we will catch our flights to Australia.' I reply.

'Haven't you people heard that there is a war in Iraq? I would not like to be flying on any planes with all this trouble going on.' And on that cheerful note he opens the boom and waves us through.

'Those are my thoughts exactly.' I widen my eyes, sighing. Gary's face folds into amused wrinkles.

'We will all be fine' Mikaela leans forward patting me on the shoulder. 'Mum, in two days time we will have an Australian visa stamped into our passports. You and Dad can then think about your future. But hell, it is a long time we will be in the air and mostly over the ocean,' she adds with another wicked chuckle. 'You can swim.' Her long finger finds the fleshy part between my ribs, and I jump.

'Shut up, Mikaela. That is not funny.' I laugh.

'I am looking forward to seeing what a first world country is all about.'

'I don't think I will be able to move to Oz if the old folks can't come, Gary. Anyway, let's go and have a look and see what is on offer for us. I don't want to think about that right now.'

'Every little thing gonna be alright.' He sings tunelessly, drumming his fingers on the steering wheel.

'Oh, Dad, don't give up your day job.' Ben laughs. 'I am going to learn how to surf. Maybe become a beach bum. Smoke a little weed.'

'Aren't you a funny boy, Ben?' I am amused as he is so full of determination to succeed that the thought of Ben ever becoming anything other than successful has never entered my head.

We eventually join the stack over Sydney, and our first view of this amazing city is seen through the clouds, a blurred haze of golden warmth lying below us. It is a perfect landing and once back on terra firma I feel my heart pumping with excitement. We float off the plane marvelling at the strange warm smells and distinct Aussie accents. Once I have the visa stamp in my passport, an intense relief floods over me, and I fight back the tears that threaten to spill. Looking up, I realize that my family are all doing exactly the same thing; staring at the open page in their hands oblivious to the people coming and going. We now have some choices in life.

Gary's sister Wool and her family are there to meet us. A festive mood and high-spirited laughter fills the air like champagne bubbles vibrating, and exploding with energetic gusto. We are absolutely exhausted but determined to get through the day. Our first couple of nights are spent at the Yacht club overlooking Sydney Harbour, a glimmering scene of golden and yellow reflections broken into fragments as the evening breeze scatters them into never-ending ripples. Through the open window, traffic sounds and laughter float over the water, drifting harmoniously with an encore of music from the iconic Sydney Opera House.

I lean on the window sill, enjoying the pleasure of unhurried moments and pinch myself gently on the wrist to ensure that this is not all a glorious dream. 'I hate Mugabe. He must go.' I shout out into the night. Gary comes rushing through from the bathroom.

'What on earth are you doing?' He looks bemused.

'It's a free country and for the first time in my life I can say what I want.' I lean out the window again. 'I hate Mugabe. He is a dictator. He needs to be taken to The Hague, and made to answer for all the Matabele people he murdered.' I shout again. Turning from the window, I rub my hands together. Ben and Mikaela are peering around the door, their eyebrows raised in amusement. 'Right, now I feel quite liberated having got that off my chest.' I burst out laughing at their stunned expressions. To the right of our room is the magnificent bridge, and I turn back to watch the endless stream of traffic twinkling across this amazing structure; majestic and proud against the dark sky. The next few days pass in a blur of cultural tours, tasty food, too much wine and many memorable moments.

A perfect holiday is turning into what can only be described as an amazing experience against a backdrop of glorious golden days and star studded evenings. I wake on the first morning on Wool's farm, to the sun streaming through our window, bathing the room in delicious warmth and adding to the comfort of stretching in a lazy catlike fashion. The aroma of coffee wafts through from the kitchen enticing me to leave the warmth of my bed and the warble of the birds tantalise and tease me. I throw on some clothes before venturing out. We sit on the front steps sipping our coffee like two sun worshipers seduced by the warmth.

'Wow, this is just beautiful, Gary.' I breathe in the fresh country air, watching the Arab horses cavorting in the paddock of succulent green grass. 'Oh my word, and so are they. Look at their arched necks and high tail plumage.' I am pointing towards these magnificent animals with their tails flowing out behind them; noble and proud creatures. The warm molasses smell of horses drifts up on the breeze bringing back memories of our 'equine friends' from home but today is not to be wasted on sad thoughts. I sit gazing at the scene before me; the rolling green fields of grass, the gum trees and not a soul in sight for as far as the eye can see. There is no beating of drums and angry voices. The morning shadows dance as opposed to the shadows back home. They cower.

'I think we have forgotten what life is all about.' I snuggle up against him. We wait for the onslaught of laughter and excited voices from the bedroom where our Ben, Mikaela and cousin Ben had polished off a couple of bottles of wine last night. I am not sure what time they had eventually put their heads down; but hunger pangs will chase them out into the fresh air. I cannot find anything negative about this vast countryside, except the spiders. We treat each new day with excitement before our couple of weeks is up.

We fly from Brisbane to Perth, and only then do we get an idea of how enormous Australia is. My cousin Wendy and Rusty pick us up at the airport and it is wonderful to bridge the years, and to spend time with their delightful children. I have many cousins in Western Australia and I feel privileged to be able to catch up with them all. As the weeks fly past, both Gary and I relax, letting go, and enjoying having this precious time with Mikaela and Ben. We laugh our way through the coppery days. The only problem with our Australian visa is that I have been told at the Embassy that only one parent will be able to relocate with us. This is because I have two siblings in Africa. We have wandered into another world, and I feel a painful stretching of my heart. What do I do? Over here, I have been far from the memories of home.

Before we know it, we are boarding the plane in Perth and on route back to Johannesburg. After a smooth flight we land back in Africa. I am longing and dreading getting home.

Driving slowly over Beitbridge, which spans the Limpoppo River, we park our truck and walk into the Zimbabwean Customs Office. The scruffy government building frowns over the car park. It is a sure sign of the sad state of affairs in our country. We cannot help but compare this to the cleanliness of the Australian countryside and buildings. The peeling paint on the buildings, trash on the pavement and the ragged street children offering to look after the car is a reminder that we are home. The tension and impatience of the people queuing to have their passports stamped is palpable. The heat in the customs office is claustrophobic. The flies hover, their buzzing amplified in the confined building. On leaving the enclosed customs area, we negotiate our way through long queues running parallel to the road; all waiting for fuel. We are grateful that we have filled the vehicle on the South African side.

Our time away has been tremendous. However, we are pleased to get home. We have returned rested and re-energized. The dogs greet us with enthusiasm, puffing excitedly with pink tongues lolling out and stumpy tails wagging madly. That evening we flop into our chairs, chatting and laughing about our holiday and with the dogs settled at my feet, we feel like we have never been away.

'What to do?' We have serious decisions to make regarding our future, and to meet the criteria of our Australian visa, we will need another four years to move money out of the country. We will then need to go out and make things happen. 'What to do?' Our visa will allow us entry into the country in a time slot of the next five years.

Chapter 32

FAREWELL TEARS

We have been home a couple of weeks and our Australian trip feels like a distant and wonderful dream; memories of endless laughter and warm times spent with family. Ben and Rich (my nephew) are as twitchy as two excited pups about their new venture. They are on countdown for their big adventure into the wide world. We had bought a rucksack in Johannesburg for each of them, and Ben has packed and unpacked his for about three days now. Clothes crawl out over his bed, spilling onto the floor; allowing only a glimpse here and there of the blue duvet cover wrestling for prime position on the unmade bed. Eventually the colourful mess of jumbled garments slip into the yawning jaws of the rucksack, which now sits squat and heavy behind the door. There are a few remaining clothes crumpled in a pile by the door. This is a reminder to me that our lives are yet again, a forever changing cycle. Excitement swirls around this young man, who has only begun to taste life as he whistles and hums his way through the days prior to him leaving. He floats on a cloud of euphoria, eyes sparkling like a thousand tiny stars as he gives us last minute instructions. He empties out the cubby hole before patting the bonnet of the green Mazda twin cab tenderly, sorry to leave his prized possession behind.

'Look after my car please, Mum. I don't want you climbing pavements in her.' His voice is gentle as he looks at me with a cheeky grin. I swot him playfully over the head, laughing at how he has manoeuvred the ownership of the vehicle into his name.

'Car rental for the year that has gone can be paid into our bank account, Ben.' I stare at him and he arches his dark eyebrows and I am unable to keep a straight face, feeling my mouth twitching. 'We are going to miss you.'

'I will miss you guys too, and my car.' He lightens the mood. They are both leaving for the UK and while it is tremendously exciting for them, it is eight thousand two hundred and thirty four kilometres from home. Gary, Ben and I all know that he will not be coming back to live in Zimbabwe. I am a vortex of emotions, swirling through the days that are now whizzing past with unrelenting haste. The thought of only seeing the boys in a years' time assaults me with a stomach-turning weightlessness that no amount of antacids can cure.

'Bye, Ben.' Adam solemnly shakes his hand. 'Be a good boy.' The simplicity of the statement is endearing. Adam has been worrying about him going to this unknown country far away from home where there is cold white stuff called snow. Ben leans over and pops one of his favourite caps on Adam's head.

'I will be a good boy, Adam.' Ben grins and I dig him in the ribs.

'Remember that statement, okay.'

We sit chatting at the airport restaurant and my sister Sue and I have silly smiles plastered across our faces. 'I feel like a clown, Sue.' I whisper in her ear and point at the smile that does not quite reach the eyes and cause bone aching jaw and tension headaches.

'Oh, Jen, I am so happy for them and so sad for us. They are not going to come back are they?'

'I don't think so.' I shake my head. 'We can't wait for you guys to get on that plane. We will have the green truck back and food on the table and a tidy house,' I playfully punch Ben on the shoulder, and he grins back smoothing out imaginary creases on his sleeve. Sue looks away, hiding her face and the tears that glisten, threatening to spill over.

We have given Ben our debit card and Gary laughingly pulls his leg 'We don't want you buying a car, Ben. Draw out the money for you and Rich and then cut the card okay.'

'I don't think that is a good idea, Dad. That is not good for our father/son relationship. What do you think, Rich? We could hit the London night spots and I want to see Scotland, Ireland and possibly travel to Europe. In fact, Rich, where would you like to go? We could have a ball.' Ben's eyes twinkle with a wicked gleam and he pats his top pocket possessively, feeling for his wallet that holds the precious debit card. 'I could get used to having this card in my wallet.'

'I'll come and find you.' Gary laughs. 'I'll hunt you both down.' This last bit of teasing is as the boys are disappearing through to Customs. 'Travel safely.'

'We will. Bye.' They can't keep the bounce out of their steps. They hand over their passports before turning back with huge grins and a wave of the hand. Suddenly they have gone and I am standing on tip toes and craning my neck like a tortoise trying to get a last glimpse of our two special young men. We all stand, huddled together for comfort, picking at imaginary threads on our clothes; trying to maintain an inner peace amongst innards that feel as if they are on the brink of a revolution. Mikaela is quiet, and as the boys disappear through to customs, her shoulders droop. She is a figure of loneliness with arms folded, hugging her sadness and a touch of envy to herself. I pop my arm around her, running a finger gently across her damp cheek.

'Oh, Mum.' She crumples, crying softly, with dignity. 'I am going to miss them. I don't think they are going to come home again.'

We watch from the balcony as the plane taxies out onto the runway, huge and powerful. I wonder if the boys can see us as they taxi past. We are a desolate looking group; all eyes on the plane. As the huge powerful machine revs up the engines, moving forward, we all as a group lean over the rail. I am clutching at my breath, holding it tight as the plane gathers momentum and takes off leaving the runway. I watch as it climbs high into the silence of the star filled heavens and becomes another twinkling light before disappearing into the impenetrable night. A huge and raucous cheer fills the balcony accompanied with wolf whistles and toy toying as the African people clap and laugh with excitement. They too have family and friends on the plane. I can feel the huge familiar lump as big as a king size apple in my throat, choking me. An arm falls around my shoulders and I feel the familiar warmth, like a comfortable coat easing my tension.

Our house is too quiet, too tidy and the food stays put in the fridge. No tell tale explosion of bread crumbs decorate the kitchen counter. No sign of chocolate wrappers in the washing machine. We all miss him but we still have Mikaela close. I have all the students who are passing through my class; and I am happy. We get on with living.

Chapter 33

LAST AFTERNOON OF SANITY

July creeps past and I am relieved when August blows in with gusty aplomb, dispersing the gloom of winter and bringing bright sunny days and chilly evenings. It has been a long freezing term, and the girls are like walking flu viruses. I am spending my last afternoon of term in the art room. The girls flutter around, as busy as house sparrows, tidying away the terms work, tucking paintings away, emptying lockers. I am busy with a feather duster, blowing away intricate lace cobwebs that cling stubbornly below the window sills, belying their delicate look.

I listen to the excited chatter and a cosy feeling comes over me. While I have been seeking renewal of my restless spirit, these girls have been a sure cure for my melancholy. They will all be going home tomorrow and there is an electric buzz in the air, contagious excitement that reverberates around the room, bouncing off the walls and infecting us all.

The high spirited hum of girls giggling is a delightful and happy sound reminding me of water burbling and gurgling over rocks as it flows uninhibited downstream. I pop my head through the door, laughing as they jostle each other while gathering their belongings and then with a cheery bye they disappear out the door. The sound of laughter fades as they disappear through the archway of the main building.

I sit for a moment staring out at the huge hockey field; the tic tic sound of the irrigation sprinklers is rhythmic and calming. I have been feeling like I am drifting through the days like a tree without roots. I love my teaching but I am worrying about the farm where

Gary is growing flowers. There have been a few rumbles of discontent. I watch as the fine spray of water mists over the field beckoning the sun to come out of hiding from behind the cloud. I narrow my eyes concentrating, holding my breath and then there it is, the most magical rainbow shimmering through the spray, hues so perfect and intense. It arcs in a glorious fusion of colours over the green grass. I idly wonder about the pot of gold at the end of the rainbow, laughing quietly to myself, feeling a deep sense of joy having witnessed this phenomenon. This is one of nature's little miracles in all its glory and a fitting farewell to the excited girls who only have one more night before they depart for their holidays. I love being here in the quiet afternoon sun and I realise that I feel safe, inside the school gates.

I grab my bag, lock the door behind me and climb into my car. I feel pretty good as I have not had a cigarette for a few weeks. I turn the tape cassette up and singing along with Cher, I try to match her deep rich voice as I head for home.

I greet Adam as he opens the gate and after parking the car, I bang the door closed before bounding up the steps and into the kitchen. The house is peaceful, save the gentle hum of the fridge. I wander through to the dining room turning on a light. Throwing my school bag on the dining room table, I glance around the lounge. The soft glow from the lamps enhances the warmth of the polished parquet flooring, the soft green furnishings and patterned throw. Reflections bounce off the shiny wooden carvings and the large mirror over the fire mantel leads the eye over the pictures and wall hangings; all lending a comfortable and welcoming feel, tying the room together. I run my hand lovingly over the old piano that used to belong to my Gran. It is a handsome instrument standing tall and proud against the far wall, the two brass candle holders gleaming in the soft light. On a table under the window a huge glass vase full of fresh flowers nods gently as I swirl past them, stopping for a quick smell and enjoying the fresh fragrance of warmer weather.

After a long soak in a hot bath, I wrap myself in a huge soft towel enjoying the hush of early evening and the quiet serenity. Wearing my silk pyjamas, I stroll back through to the lounge, gazing at the old wooden chiming clock sitting on the mantle above the fire place. Gary should be home any minute.

I strike a match holding it carefully under the dry grass, wrinkling my nose and sneezing as the sulphur tickles my sinuses. A puff of smoke billows out with a whoosh and I reach over for the ancient leather bellows, creased and bloated like an old textured relief map. The flame takes hold and I sit back stretching my legs out towards the warmth.

Gary pours us a drink when he gets home, and using his foot he nudges the dogs to move from their prime position on the mat in front of the fire. He crouches down and feeds the fire with more logs. The orange red glow of the flames dances rhythmically as they lick up and around the logs, sizzling and spluttering loudly in the quiet of the lounge. It is not long before the red hot coals are radiating cosy warmth. The dogs creep back onto their mat as Gary stands and eases his body onto a chair on the other side of fire place.

'This is so idyllic, Gary, a log fire, end of term and a whole month to garden. I can't think of anything more perfect.' I sigh with contentment. 'How are things out at Churchill Farm?' Gary tells me about his day and I turn to him with a chuckle as he loves the challenge of growing the hypericum berries. His face is tanned and glowing. Deep laughter lines furrow and roll around his eyes which are the deep brown of pecan shells, black flecks reflecting the glow from the roaring fire.

Chapter 34

THE DARK

I turn on the TV flipping channels until the 'Queen of mean' comes on. 'Should we watch Anne Robinson tear strips of some poor bugger tonight, Gary?' I bend down to scratch Toffee on her back. She pricks her ears, listening intently and growling softly. I am watching her closely and turn to Gary with an enquiring look. 'What do you think she's growling at?' I laugh. 'I don't think she likes Anne Robinson's voice.'

'Who can blame her? It is most certainly Anne's voice. My word, she can be such a bitch.' Toffee stretches out again, allowing me to scratch her vulnerable soft under belly. I lean over her to pop another log on the fire when she starts growling again, a deep baritone in her chest. With the hackles on her neck raised like an angry porcupine, she sniffs the air, tasting it. She walks stiff legged towards the passage door. I turn the TV down and both Gary and I sit, ears cocked, listening intently. We hear nothing but the crackling of the fire and the loud ticking from the clock; nothing untoward.

I feel the hair on the nape of my neck prickle and I shiver as a cool menacing air brushes my skin. A feeling of impending disaster has a million butterflies flapping helplessly in my stomach. I jump when Beano, with a low throaty growl joins Toffee at the door. Gary and I are not far behind them. He pulls the door wide open and the hush of early evening explodes in a frenzy of blurred fists and boots. Toffee and Beano squeal in pain; the sound claws at my heart.

Every muscle in my body shrieks at me to flee, but for precious seconds I remain frozen and unable to comprehend what I am seeing. Gary is on the floor screaming like a wounded animal.

'Jen... run.' Four or five African men are holding him captive. Angry boots and fists are finding their mark on his body.

I turn and run, but I have wasted precious seconds and get no further than the fireplace across the room towards the kitchen. I scream as the huge man grabs me by my hair tugging me back and I feel a warm trickle down my legs. Through the murk, I can hear the dogs yelping and Gary screaming for him to leave me alone. The pungent smell of urine invades my senses, constricting my throat and I am helpless as his hands go around my neck, thumbs pressing on my windpipe and squeezing tightly. I struggle to breathe. Losing my slipper as he drags me across the room, my eyes bulging and I am totally at his mercy. My mind swirls as a void of darkness pulls me. Down, down into the quiet.

In the distance I hear Gary screaming, distorted drawn out sounds echoing. Suddenly I am clawing at his hands using my nails as weapons gouging, desperate and fighting back. He throws me, and like a rag doll I crash uncoordinated and floppy, banging my head on the table and jarring my spine. I lie gasping; wheezing in agony as I take ragged breaths trying to fill my lungs. The room spins in slow motion; a nightmare of psychedelic circles and shooting stars. I am aware of a distorted figure looming over me raising his arm and instinctively I cover my head, cowering. The wooden hippo crashes onto my arm and I recoil in pain aware of a high pitched primeval scream, and then realise the awful eerie sound is coming from me. The hot smell of his stale cigarette breath assaults my nostrils, instantaneously invoking my gag reflex and I lean over retching; spittle dribbling down my chin. Gary is still shouting as I am dragged to my feet, clutching my arm and gasping. My teeth rattle and I am aware of a continual thud, meaty sounds and the coppery taste of blood floods my mouth. My rings have been ripped off my hands, nails on flesh, tearing the skin. I concentrate, trying to clear my head. The dark shadowy figures are all moving in slow motion, swirling mists of violence. There are seven of them. The gang leader is standing over Gary, waving his arm and I catch sight of a pistol. My stomach constricts in fear as he appears to float towards me.

'Go back to Britain you fucking white bitch. You do not belong here in Zimbabwe.' he screams, hot spittle peppering my face. 'Money! I want money. Where are you hiding your foreign currency?' I remember that I have some money from a raffle that I had done at the school.

'I have some money in the safe in the office. It is not foreign currency. It is not a lot though.' I croak, feeling my heart thudding up in my throat. 'The key for the office door is in the bedroom.'

He nods, narrowing his eyes. 'Watch him.' He screams, pointing the weapon at Gary. The man in a floral blue shirt, who had first attacked me, grabs my arm, twisting it up and around my back, steering me towards the door. I feel a hand shoving me hard between my shoulders, and I cannonball down the stairs into the passage wall, hearing a sickening crunch as I impact against a photo frame, breaking the glass. The man with the weapon pulls me up by the collar of my pyjamas, and blue shirt frogmarches me through to the bedroom. I gasp at the chaotic scene before me. Our bed has collapsed and the mattress spills over onto the floor. Draws have been turned out; clothes, broken pictures and shoes litter the carpet. My head is muzzy and I am unable to hold onto thoughts as they swirl away into the dark shadows, out of reach. My mind begs for clarity and I desperately try to remember where I put the keys to our office.

The man in the blue flower print shirt uses one of the bedsteads as a weapon. 'Hurry up and find the key.' He is empowered by this violent behaviour, aroused and dangerous. 'Joy ride white bitch, you want a joy ride?' He runs a tongue over his thick lips, eyes glistening as he gyrates obscenely with his hips; the threat and meaning very clear.

My stomach churns with fear as he prods me, provoking me. Like a miracle I catch a glint and leaning over I pick up the keys holding them in my palm. 'Thank God.' I am thinking as I hold it towards him, hands trembling as I keep my eyes downcast; subservient. I hope the keys will get his mind off other things. He snatches them with greedy fingers enclosing them in his palm and marches me forward towards the office. He holds the key out and with shaking fingers I fight with the lock, trying desperately to control the trembling and aware of the eyes burning into my back. As the lock clicks open he pushes me away, holding me against the wall. With one hand pushing against my chest, he leans into the cupboard, his eyes scanning the contents of the shelf, avariciously. Greedy fingers enclose over the bag of money I have collected from the raffle for the art room and he hugs it to his chest, turning to me with a malicious grin. He pulls me towards his bulging groin. 'Joy ride you Bitch. I want a joy ride'.

'You must take my Mercedes.' I croak. My mind is reeling and my insides are recoiling in horror. I take him through to the dining room table where I have left my keys, and turn my bag upside down, before rifling through the pockets. My only defence is to play ignorant, and my brain is telling me not to scream, as this will excite him further. All I know is that I would rather die than be raped by this bastard.

They work in shifts; some are beating us while the others move our belongings onto the truck; all this coming and going is causing confusion. The man in the blue floral shirt is never far from me; a menacing dark shadowy figure as he holds me captive. I view him through downcast eyes, weighed down with fear; swollen and half closed. He continues to harass me as he prods and pushes me back towards the bedroom. Gary has a look of absolute horror, his eyes narrowing with pain and fear, but powerless to come to my aid as they keep beating him. I estimate that they have been in our house for about an hour and a half and I plead with the man in control.

'You must go now as the guard at the gate will be calling for help'. He eventually barks an order to the others.

The guy wearing the blue shirt drags me out of our room and into the family bathroom, pushing me onto the floor before tying me up. I keep my eyes on the floor as he loops the rope around my ankles, cutting the blood supply as he pulls tightly, making me flinch. He then does the same to my wrists, securing them behind my back. I can hear Gary shouting my name. He is frantic with fear and I close my eyes, shivering uncontrollably as the muffled thuds and groans continue as he keeps on relentlessly shouting for me. Suddenly I feel this warm body next to me and Toffee is cowering and leaning into me, trembling in terror as she pushes her warm nose against my neck, nudging me. I am so grateful to have her close and I feel hot salty tears rolling down my cheeks. I am muttering 'just take them away please' over and over again.

The man in the blue shirt swaggers back in and kneeling close to me he runs his hands slowly over my body, the sound of his breathing, loud and rasping in my ear. His hot breath ruffles my hair. My heart pounds against my ribs and I am sure that he must be aware of the thudding sounds in the silence. I feel myself retching and trickles of perspiration run down between my shoulder blades leaving my pyjama top damp. I am frantic with panic. I try to dampen my lips with a tongue that feels glued to the roof of my mouth, and wince as he leans over me feeling under my legs and bum. He straightens up staring at me through heavy hooded eyes and I lower my look quickly. He is looking for my mobile phone and I hold my breath in, breathing out slowly trying to still my pounding heart. With a last kick at Toffee and another one aimed at me he finally leaves.

The house breathes silently. I sit with my back against Toffee, head cocked to one side listening intently and trying to marshal my thoughts. The darkness is heavy. All I can hear is my ragged breaths.

'Jen are you there?' I realise that Gary is tied up in the room next to me. He is tapping on the wall between us.

'Shush,' I whisper back. I am so scared that blue shirt will return. We both sit in silence. I hear the truck start up and wheel spinning noisily, one of our assailants' revs out of the property, hitting the gate with a loud crunching crash before roaring up the road. I manage to get my hands free and am trying to untie my legs as Gary appears from around the corner and folds me into his arms.

'Oh my God! Gary. Are you okay?' I put my finger to his swollen bloodied lips. 'What have they done to you?' His face is full of blood and all I can think about are his previous head injuries.

'Shush, Jen. I don't know if they have all gone.' He pats Toffee and we decide that our best bet is to get out of the house. We clamber out through the window with its mangled burglar bar, easing through gently and dropping to the ground with a loud thud. We crouch down in the flower bed, taking cover behind an elephant ear, frantically searching for signs of life. It is eerily quiet. Dark clouds are towering up over the garden. The moon sends out a cold shaft of light deceiving me, playing tricks on my eyes with outsized shapes that sway and gyrate in the shadows. Gary nudges me. There is no movement or noise and so we dash across the driveway, aware of how loud our footsteps sound as we crash through the flowerbed scattering petals in our wake. Jumping up onto the roof of the Mercedes, we climb over the wall, dropping into our neighbour's flower bed. Once in the safety of John Van Reenen's garden we both open our mouths and hollow for him, banging loudly on the back door and causing a loud furore. John's two dogs take umbrage to our evening visit and snip at our heels. Their repeated growling and barking eventually alerts him. He opens his back door and stares at us both. It takes a second or two for him to register the state we are in and suddenly his eyes widen in horror and he beckons us into the kitchen.

'What the hell guys. Jees, what on earth... what on earth has happened? The bloody bastards. Who did this to you?' He is visibly agitated as his eyes flash from Gary to me shaking his head and muttering angrily. He pours a couple of neat brandies into glasses and hands one to each of us. 'Come through to the lounge.' He gently propels us through to the lounge.

Glynis (John's wife) pops her head around the lounge door 'Oh my goodness.' Her hands fly to her face. She rushes over to me. 'Who on earth has done this to you?' She whispers. 'Come and sit down both you.'

'I can't sit down. I have wet myself.' I feel a wave of embarrassment lurching high into my throat and then it is gone, and tears leak out and down my cheeks. Glynis lends me some tracksuit pants. After phoning our friends Paul and Mags, we sit down and in shaky voices answer all the questions that John and Glynis throw at us. Paul and Mags take less than five minutes to arrive.

'Jesus wept.' Her eyes fill with tears. 'What on earth?' She can't finish the question, taking a glass of brandy from John. Once we have finished our story, we down another warm amber tot of brandy and I pinch one of John's smokes, inhaling deeply. I cough and splutter as the nicotine touches the back of my throat, but I am too shaken up to worry about what I am doing.

'I am concerned about Gary's head. I think he needs to see a Doctor.' I peer at them all through eyes that are swollen and bloody.

George, our doctor has left the country and so we see Dr. Martin. He examines me gently prodding and pulling, shaking his head as I pull away in pain. My wrist is swollen but there are no broken bones. I find I have many tender spots all over my battered body. He examines Gary's head and apart from nicks and cuts he is fine. His lower back and sides are going to bruise badly. We are both given an anti-tetanus injection and after thanking Dr. Martin for coming to the hospital to see us, we climb back in Paul's truck. We have already decided that we will sleep in their spare room.

'My dogs, Gary and Paul, please we need to make sure they are okay. I am worried about Beano.' On the way back to our house, we come across them, two forlorn shadows crouching under skies that are black and quivering with anger. It is time to be afraid again. I burst into tears. Paul and Gary take them back to the house, check them over and lock them up in the courtyard.

Chapter 35

THE FEAR

Dark sinister forces invade my mind causing me to cry out in desperation. I sit up banging my head against the wall, wrenching my tee shirt off my body. I am bathed in sweat. Sinking back into the depths of the duvet, I curl up into a tight ball shivering uncontrollably. The decaying atmosphere wraps around me, constricting my breathing and I sit up with my heart pounding, cocking my head and listening intently. I run a trembling hand through my hair that hangs like clumpy combs of seaweed. I can hear a scraping noise.

The clock chimes three, four and eventually five. Shards of sunlight slice through the slit in the curtain cutting Gary's face in two. I gasp as I stare down on the purple hue smeared across his swollen lids and leaking down onto his cheeks. Feeling my gaze, he opens his eyes, peering at me through a road map of broken veins. My bottom lip trembles and tears escape from between bloodied eyelashes. A feeling of grief covers me like a thick choking blanket and I cry with great gasping sobs as Gary holds me tenderly in his bruised arms.

'Let it out.' I can feel his warm breath caressing my neck as he places a light kiss on the mauve stain at the base of my skull. Climbing out of bed, I am stiff and sore and rear back in shock as I catch sight of my face in the mirror; I look macabre. One eye is glued together with dried blood. And so I gape at the strange image peering back at me through the other half closed eye.

'Oh, Gary, look at me.' I croak. 'Look at you. We look like something out of a horror movie.' My tongue is glued to the roof of my mouth and the metallic taste in the back of my throat is strong. The taste is a stark reminder of the horror of the evening before.

Throwing on my tee shirt, I drag on some jeans and we go through to the lounge and pour ourselves a cup of coffee, sipping and swallowing, but not tasting the bitter strong flavour.

Mikaela and Sue bustle in. Sue shakes her blonde head, her face crumpling. 'The bastards! What have they done to you both?' She sobs, wrapping her arms gently around me. Our tears mingle together as Mikaela, laces her hands, cracking her knuckles loudly.

'Oh, Mum.' She cries. The four of us stand huddled together. Mikaela wets a piece of cotton wool and gently removes the blood clots from my eyelashes.

'Hold still, Mum. I don't want to hurt you.'

'Thanks, Mikaela.' I rasp painfully, wincing as she takes my arm. 'We need to go and see mum and dad.' I turn to Paul and Mags. 'Thanks guys.' There is no need for any more than that. Gary and I wait in the car while Sue and Mikaela go inside the little cottage to speak to mum and dad and to warn them that we are both black and blue. These two old folk rush out to the car and ferry us both inside; mum making clucking noises as she busies herself making tea and toast. Dad paces like a caged lion, his face like a storm cloud as he growls deeply in his throat.

John Van Reenen had contacted the Police the evening before and they phone Gary requesting entry into the house. The dogs are pathetically pleased to see us. I run my hands over both bitches, feeling the lumps and bumps that ripple in pain beneath my palms. Kneeling down gingerly I allow both dogs to bury their heads in my lap, while I whisper soothingly into their ears.

Edna and Adam are hovering. They don't know how to cope with the feeling of unease that has settled over the property like thick smothering fog. Ben who is far from the memories of home is distressed beyond reason with this latest news. I have assured him that we will be fine, but deep inside, I am not so sure.

The thought of walking back into the chaos is terrifying and I stand glued to the spot, gripping the door jams with chalk white fingers. The coppery stagnant aftertaste floods my mouth warning me of impending panic. Crunching Gary's fingers tightly, we walk through the kitchen door into the aftermath of last night's visitors.

'Oh my God, Gary, look what they have done.' I stare in horror at the scene before me, clasping my hand over my mouth. I cannot believe that it was only twelve hours before that I had viewed this same room, marvelling at the warmth and ambience. Photograph frames, cushions, ornaments, broken wooden side tables, smashed glass table and other oddments scatter the floor space. The large vase of flowers has been smashed and they lie, wilting and crushed. Fallen flower blossoms, like a symbol of how fragile life can be. I rub my burning throat gently, shuddering as I recollect the feeling of not being able to breathe.

'Oh, Mum. I am so sorry.' Mikaela's eyes well with tears, her teeth nibbling gently on her bottom lip. The eerie quiet is broken by the clock chiming ten, and we all jump nervously. Tension and fear pulsates through my veins. I beg for normality. The throw lies, discarded, torn and stained with blood. A vulnerable sad pile and no amount of washing will restore it to its former luxurious glory. We crunch our way through the room and follow the chaos that spills out and down the stairs towards the bedroom. Papers, documents and books are strewn down the passage and the soft glow of the light is at odds with the pictures and photographs that hang at odd angles looking down on the mess below.

The whirlwind of chaos continues into the bedroom and I gasp, holding my cheeks and shaking my head at the broken bed frame. The whole scene reminds one of the after effects from a tornado. Clothes, bedding and drawers have been thrown around the room with careless abandon. The cupboard doors are wide open. I step gingerly over an old jersey crying sharply as I snag my toe on a ragged piece of pine wood lying in wait and camouflaged under my camel coloured skirt that had been bought in Australia. The plight of my toe is momentarily forgotten as I scoop up my favourite skirt holding it lovingly to my body, caressing the soft material between my fingers before dropping it back on top of the pile.

'Imagine that, Gary. They must have missed this in their haste.' I feel pathetically relieved before thinking 'how bizarre'. There are no more hidden treasures in the cupboard. The metal hanging rail houses countless empty hangers and they sway gently as I run my fingers over them, tinkling quietly. Sue weeps. I jump nervously as the dogs bark angrily and we pick our way through the mess, stepping carefully in case off any hidden obstacles and broken shards of glass, we make our way back to the kitchen.

A tall slim policeman is leaning with one thin arm resting on the polished dining room table. His fingers are beating a rhythmic tattoo and I find I am staring at his manicured fingernails; pinky white against his dark skin. His closeness makes me uncomfortable and I keep my eyes downcast as I fidget with a small hole in my blue tracksuit top, trying to control the nausea that has my throat closing and the room spinning. His short curly hair is tinged with grey and he surveys us both through narrowed unfriendly eyes giving me the impression that he is not on our side with this investigation. I listen to the soft spoken voice and I feel small beads of perspiration forming under my hairline. I am aware of a strong odour, slightly sweet and mingled with sweat. Putting my hand out to steady myself, I sink onto the soft green cushion, resting my head in my palms and Gary touches me gently on my damp neck and they move away. Thankfully I can close my eyes while rubbing my aching temples with stiff swollen ring less fingers. Sue and Mikaela take up their positions; one on each side of me like two tawny haired lionesses, vigilant and angry. The soft spoken policemen introduces me to two more officers and I sit waiting patiently while they poke around through our belongings on the pretence of gathering evidence. They do not take any fingerprints and eventually leave. I expel a huge breath, blowing the air over my face to cool the perspiration, sighing with relief.

I need to scrub my hair and skin as I feel vulnerable and soiled. 'Gary, did I have my pyjama pants on when we climbed over the wall to Johns?' I ask him quietly, my voice trembling and gruff. 'I have blanks of what happened last night. I feel so dirty and itchy and that blue shirt would not let me alone. Are you sure I had my pj pants on?'

Gary's voice is gentle as he reassures me, wrapping his arm around my shoulders. 'Of course you had your pj pants on, Jen.' I lean into him and we stare at each other's battered faces before I turn and run a bath. Lying back I arch my neck, wetting my hair before pouring the fresh smelling lemon shampoo into my hand. I scrub my body with the sponge, trying to erase the memory of rough hands shoving me through the silk of my pyjamas. After finding a pair of jeans under the bedding, I pull them up carefully over my bruised legs. Having scrubbed my teeth and gargled with some salt water to rid my mouth of the coppery blood taste, I join my family, who are standing, patiently waiting outside the bathroom door. We leave Gary to soak in a hot bath.

All my jewellery, our clothes, passports, documents and all electrical goods have gone. Gary's company truck has been stolen. They had not taken the Mercedes and we soon realise the reason why; the fuel gauge is on empty.

Chapter 36

AFTERMATH

This violent incident has a major impact on me. Five weeks later the bruising is disappearing fast but my fear is alive and kicking. It is the kind of fear that eats you up from your insides. Those men know who we are. They are nameless faces.

We are not sure why we were chosen, but we do feel sure that we were deliberate targets. Gary had been called through to Harare a couple of days before our burglary to attend a meeting with an official from the Government Department of Lands and Resettlement Office. Sitting opposite a well fed middle aged man whose crinkled suit is straining at the seams, thoughts of a certain 'Government valuator' had come to mind. With a pudgy hand holding a gold parker pen, he fiddled with his tight curls, tugging them gently before writing the offer onto a piece of paper. His chair creaked mournfully as he leant forward pushing the paper across the desk to Gary. Gary's laughter was scornful as he glanced at the paper. The offer for Methven Ranch was ridiculous, better than the value of a basin, but we could have sold our Mercedes Benz for more; even with eighty thousand kilometres on the clock. The official scraped the floor loudly as he pushed back his chair, terminating the meeting with an angry scowl and folding his arms over his pendulous belly. He dismissed Gary with an angry wave. We will never know if that meeting and our armed attack had anything in common.

After a week of sleeping away from the house, it is time to face my fears. Our neighbour John Van Reenen has been absolutely fantastic; arranging for a burglar alarm system to be put in. People are supportive, popping in and making sure we are both okay.

I fight my demons every night. I am eaten up by fear as soon as the evening closes in and the darkness fills my mind. I pour a large drink. Sitting at the dining room table playing cards one evening, I hear a noise and my insides freeze. The noises are coming from behind the locked passage door. (We have kept it locked since our robbery). I feel the hairs on the nape of my neck prickle and I let out a high pitched scream before running into the kitchen. Gary grabs a large carving knife, the bone handle edging out from his palm.

'Please don't open the door, Gary.' I am screaming from the kitchen, my heart lurching violently up the back of my throat.

'Jen, be quiet and lock yourself in the kitchen.' He puts his finger to his lips, leaving the room. However, I am right behind him. He slowly pads across the lounge, hesitating at the door and unaware of my shadow clinging to his back. As he turns the key in the lock, I hold my breath, exhaling loudly as he pushes the door open. Our black cat Felix comes strolling through purring like a miniature engine. Weaving in and out of Gary's legs and unaware of the tension he has caused, Gary turns with a startled expression on his face when he sees me. Lowering the knife, our eyes meet.

'I thought I asked you to stay in the kitchen.' I stand with my arms wrapped around my body, my heart pounding so loud and my mouth open. My breathing is jagged and I stare at him as a boiling cauldron of emotion erupts, bursting upwards from my stomach, burning my throat and stinging my eyes as the tears spill over and down my cheeks. Covering my face with fingers that are shaking I stand still, shoulders drooped and I sob, loud cries of anguish.

'I can't go on living here anymore Gary. We have got to move. I feel like I am going to lose my mind,' I plead with him, taking huge deep breaths, swallowing and hiccupping as I try to control myself.

He hugs me tight. 'We will organise our lives, Jen. I just need to think about how we are going to play this.' I nod, burrowing into his shoulder. 'I have not wanted to tell you this, but I received a death threat last week.'

'You....what?' I stammer, fear, my familiar friend clutching my heart. 'You are being serious aren't you?' I look at him.

'Jen, I would never joke about something like that. There are serious problems on the farm. I have spoken to your mum and dad. Dad is going to get his Irish passport and then at least they can make their own decisions on whether they leave Zimbabwe.'

'Where are we going to go? We can't go to Australia as we don't have enough money to satisfy our visa.' I croak. 'I have handed in my notice at the school.'

'You have? But you love it there.' I feel his warmth.

'I don't know, Gary. Everything has changed now. I am not the same person. I need to move on.'

'At least mum and dad are safer at Borrowdaille Trust, so I feel that we can now make plans for us and then if they want to follow, that is their choice.' He smiles sadly.

'What. Where are we going to go? Where can we go?' I am speechless. 'Nobody out there has shown any signs of wanting us, Gary. We are Zimbabweans, and have nowhere to go.'

'I will make enquiries, Jen. I am not sure who will want us. I do not want to go to South Africa, as I think that is jumping from the frying pan into the fire. I just need you to know that this could take months to organise.' He stares off. 'At least Dad will have his Irish passport. That will give them options.'

Mikaela has decided that she will join the boys over in the UK and I feel emptier than empty, but relieved when her plane takes off. We are setting our children free and allowing them to go and spread their wings, and to make a life for themselves. The flowers are a disaster and hyper-inflation is another hurdle to cross. Rumstock (the flower business) is winding down fast as is our personal exporting venture.

'Time to leave is now, Jen. The exchange rate is now $1 000 000, 00 Zimbabwe dollars for £1.00.'

Chapter 37

TIME TO LEAVE OUR BELOVED AFRICA

Gary and I spend many hours sitting on our rock in Gosho Park (A game park, part of the school where I taught), a rock that has become a symbol of strength for me. The feel of warm granite below my bum generates a sense of peace and calm, enabling me to think in a clear and rational way. We are surrounded by pristine Brachystegia woodlands, alive with different species of birds, all making music from the afternoon shadows. Above me the leaves sway gracefully, lulled by nature's timeless rhythms.

I turn my head and peep at Gary through half slit eyes 'Ok, Gary let's do it. I think I am ready now.' I close my eyes, heart thumping wildly at my bravery. I can smell the scent of the earth hovering in the air. 'Where will the road ahead take us?' I whisper to the trees looking down on me. In the distance, the high pitched barking of the zebra echoes on nature's soothing breeze. Gary sits up and makes a motion with his head that might be construed as a nod. We both know that the time has now come for us to make serious decisions concerning our future.

'Oh my, God, I just can't imagine not having our afternoon walk through this fantastic game park. How will we cope?' I close my eyes listening to the birds. 'But we will feel safe won't we Gary?' Negative thoughts ghost into view using the afternoon sun to hide their attack. I jump to my feet, offering Gary my hand. 'Come Gary, let's go home now. All these thoughts are putting scorpions in my brain.'

'I know the feeling, Jen. We are going to have to make a decision and do things quickly. When I am in Gosho Park, I don't want to leave, but as darkness falls and I look at the fear in your eyes, I know we have to leave.' He takes my hand, heaving himself up onto his feet. 'Come on, let's go.'

Gary has never let grass grow under his feet and after enquiries at the embassy regarding visas, he books our plane tickets. We have six weeks to organise our lives. Over the past five years, we had packed up home enough times to warrant us the title of 'experienced movers'. However nothing had prepared me for the emotional roller coaster ride that we suddenly find ourselves on, racing up and freefalling down as we balance on what feels like the edge of our future. Luckily for us, Mikaela will be home within a few days to renew her visa. I can't wait to see her sunny face.

Ever since April 2000 the days have been dark and stormy and we are both frantically swimming towards the sunlight at the end of the dark tunnel. How do you pack up twenty five years of married life into two suitcases and a few old school trunks? That is the amount of luggage that will do the transition with us. We make a pile on the lounge floor of all the 'maybe items' that can come with us. Through a process of elimination, we work our way through the huge pile, putting very few things into the trunks. All the photographs are removed from the frames and placed into the trunk and slowly over the course of the next two weeks; the rooms empty; becoming an echo of their former selves.

Gary's face reflects the same bewildered look as mine, as he packs and unpacks our sparse collection of beloved belongings that will make the journey with us. All too soon the trunks are being dropped off at the airport and the next time we see them will be in a different country.

Our garage is full of Gary's tools. Shad, our sixteen foot fishing boat which is parked in the driveway will go to our friends Andre and Laura.

After one of our long morning walks weaving through the msasa trees on the golf course, I kneel down to remove the leads off the bitches. I bury my face in my hands, the worry of what we might have to do eating into my stomach, causing the acid to burn up my throat. I notice Gary and Mikaela both watching me. The fate of my dogs eats into every waking thought of mine. Time is running out now as we have ten days left and I have still not found anyone to take of these two faithful bitches.

'Gary, please have these dogs put down.' I beg and plead with him. Mikaela turns away, leaving the room.

'No, Jen. I can't bring myself to do it. I am still hoping that someone will take them on. They are too young to be put to sleep.'

'Please.' I am fraying like a cable that is stretched too tight.

'No. I can't do it.' He looks away, frowning. 'I have had to put all our domestic animals, save these two bitches to sleep. I can't.' We are at loggerheads where they are concerned and my pleading and begging falls on deaf ears. He will not listen. Our last days are being chased by the leaving date.

Sitting out on the lawn a couple of mornings later, I sip on my tea, swallowing gently. 'I am not going to go, Gary. I have changed my mind.' My heart skips a beat.

'Sorry... what the hell do you mean?' The furrow between his eyes deepens and his irises are emotional storms.

'Just like I said, we will call the whole thing off; give Frank back the money he has paid us for the house. Find a job and just continue here and make the most of our lives.' Blue eyes meet brown ones.

'Jen, our trunks have gone. Our house is empty save some chairs and our bed, and now you are talking like some lunatic about changing the plan and not leaving. Are you bloody serious?' His voice is angry.

'No, Gary, not mad. I am just scared and sad and worried about my family and my dogs. What the hell are we going to do about Beans and Toffee? We leave this country one week today and we don't have a plan for them.' He stands up, running a hand over his tired face.

'You are bloody insane and I can't deal with you in this mood.'

'I can't deal with you either, Gary. I have changed my mind. That's all.' I burst into tears before storming into the house, my footsteps echoing on the wooden steps as I run upstairs to the bedroom. 'I am not going anymore.' I shriek, banging the door loudly.

Adam and Edna have disappeared, giving us space. I am quite sure that the whole neighbourhood are aware of the ongoing saga of the Luke's dogs. Adam has a job with mum and dad, so that is one problem that has been resolved. We have given him enough money to build a house in the communal lands, where he has managed to secure a plot. Edna is going to join her husband in South Africa as an illegal immigrant. I have not been able to dissuade her from this treacherous path.

Two more days rush past. Our conversation has not been mentioned again, but time is fast running out. I move around the rooms that echo anxiety, trying to still my rampant thoughts. I am determined that we won't go.

'I have not changed my mind, Gary.' I am halfway through packing a box of ornaments. He ignores my statement, picking up yet another box of precious items that won't be coming with us. My phone rings. 'Hello.'

'Jen, it is Lo. I have some good news for you, my friend. Mike and Laurie are going to take your dogs.' (Mike was Gary's flower partner, and he is Lo's brother.) I slump onto the carpet. 'Hey, Jen are you there?'

'Lo, I am.' My mind is spinning. This makes things so final, now we will have to go. 'Thank you so much for finding a home for the dogs.' I croak as that damn apple has lodged itself back in my throat. I put the phone down, tears streaming down my face. 'Mike and Laurie are going to take them.' I blow my nose. 'Now.... we have to go, Gary.' A small space in me is disappointed.

'I cannot think of a better home for these two bitches. I don't think they have any idea of what their decision means to us, Jen.' Gary eyes are swimming. 'They are taking these dogs unseen. How bloody fantastic are they?' We hold each other tight. 'So, are we going?' I can only nod into his shoulder.

Our last weekend in Zimbabwe towers over us. Sue and Tony have come out to spend time with us. Sue's eyes are bloodshot and stormy. She pops her arm around me before apologising, 'I just can't believe you are going and I am sorry in advance; my taps just keep leaking and you will just have to put up with me because unless you can find a good plumber, there is nothing I can do.' Her attempt at joking raises a smile.

'Sue, I am so glad you are here. The girls are going today. Gary is going to take them through to Harare this afternoon and I am feeling sick to the pit of my stomach about it. No don't bloody cry, Sue. Shit man. Oh come on please stop now'. I wipe the end of my bright red nose. We open a coke and move out onto the lawn and Sue cries again when she sees that I have put names on the collars of the two bitches.

'I had to as Laurie does not know the dogs and when she meets them, she won't know who's who.' My heart is cracking. I kneel down and both dogs come forward, plump and folding in rolls as they wiggle. I wrap my arms around these two faithful and brave dogs, my support systems over the past five years, always on my shadow, ready to give comfort with a wet nose kiss. Watching the truck leave the yard with both bitches grinning out the window, I feel as if I have been run over.

'I don't know if I can go through with this.'

'Come on, Mum; let's go for a walk on the golf course.' Sue drives us through the little village that had become home since leaving the farm, making our way to the golf course Sue's foot hits the brake, throwing me forwards as she narrowly misses a tree.

'Jees, Sue look where you're going....' I turn to her. An air of intense sadness sits heavily on her shoulders. Her mouth is tight.

'I hate the stupid fucking bastard.' She spits out a string of profanities between sobs, hitting her hands against the steering wheel. Exhausted, she leans her head on the wheel, her shoulders shaking as she weeps quietly, before controlling her wayward emotions. A silence stretches.

'Bastard.' She repeats quietly. The whole situation is surreal and I start to laugh which makes Mikaela laugh and in turn Sue. We sit there crying, laughing and calling Mugabe every awful 'bastard' name we can think of. Once the absurdity of the situation has calmed, we return home without having a walk. Saying goodbye to my sister and Tony is heartbreaking.

It is with a real heavy heart and sadness that I say goodbye to my old friend Biff.

'Oh damn, my 'pinkie promise' has been broken, Gary.'

'You broke our pact, Jen.' She cries, wiping her nose.

'I am sorry, Biff.' I hug her tight. We spend a lovely morning together talking nonstop, but after lunch it is time to leave. Biffs shoulders sag and I am aware of her tears as we hug goodbye.

We had so many difficult and emotional goodbyes to get through. My dearest old school pal Lo envelopes me in a warm hug. I return the squeeze thinking back over many years of shared laughter and memories. Ours is a special bond of friendship that started when I was fifteen, and we were both borders at high school. This bond will survive for many more years to come.

Leaving all our good friends behind is painfully hard and emotionally draining, so I hug Eelco, Maggie, Laura and Andre and we leave as quickly as possible, all the while trying to keep some sort of composure.

And then there is our trusted gardener Adam. 'Good bye, Adam. I want to thank you for all the work you have done in the gardens we have built up. Look after yourself.' My voice catches and Adam shuffles his feet, distress in every awkward movement.

'Ndatenda chaizvo, Madam.' (Many thanks) His eyes are bewildered. 'Famba zvakanaka.' (Bon voyage.)

'Chenjera tsotsi, Adam. Famba zvakanaka.' (Be careful of thieves. Go well.)

I disappear into the empty lounge, my shoulders heavy. For twenty five years, Adam has been a part of my life and I feel as if we are letting him down. He can't go anywhere. I listen to Gary wishing Adam well. And then he has gone. Twenty five years of a working relationship all ended with thanks. I sit in the bare room, my heart pounding.

Edna had left a few days ago, her future shaky and unsure as she faces a lifetime of being an illegal immigrant; given the fact that she has also been treated like a foreigner in her own country. This government has much to answer for as we all part company, abandoning the road. She cried when we said good bye. I feel sad.

On our last morning, my Dad stands, a solitary and lonely figure standing outside their back door, his skinny long legs sticking out the bottom of his dressing gown, bony hand waving goodbye. My heart lurches painfully. Mum and Mikaela are taking us to the airport.

Hugging my mum goodbye is incredibly hard. Her lined face crumples, folding down. I just do not know when we will see any of these people again. I hug Mikaela, grateful that she is there to see to Sue, Mum and Dad. I know that their hearts are bleeding.

I don't remember the long walk through customs or boarding the plane. As we taxi down the runway and lift off into the air, I feel such heart wrenching sadness, relief, fear and total bewilderment at what we are doing. We are leaving behind a life; the only kind of life we have ever known. We are leaving family and lifelong friends. The last precious minutes at the airport have passed so quickly, and I wish that we could have made time stand still; to just be able to hold onto and savour our last moments in Zimbabwe.

I crane my neck holding my breath as I press my face against the small window, peering down on my beloved sun kissed land before we are swallowed high into the sunlit silence of the vast skies. Nine hours later and we become part of the Zimbabwean diaspora.

Epilogue

Gary wakes me from my reverie 'We have arrived, Jen. Bloody traffic has been outrageous.' I gaze out of the window at the grey sky. The A43, the road to Silverstone, Northamptonshire UK is still bumper to bumper with cars. Gary has put the indicator on and in another couple of minutes and we will be leaving the traffic behind. 'Where have you been?'

'Unlocking the door of my memories and watching the films that have been hidden away in my mind, Gary.'

'Are you okay?'

'Life is a strange old thing!' I smile at him. 'What an amazing road with all its twists and turns. What a journey we have been on. I don't know what the future holds for us but our past, with all its peaks and troughs will make for interesting stories for the next generation.'

'We have most certainly arrived and now we need to make it all worthwhile.' Gary leans over, putting his hand on my knee.

'We most certainly learned how to dance in the storm.'

255

46344628R00150

Printed in Poland
by Amazon Fulfillment
Poland Sp. z o.o., Wrocław